François
TRUFFAUT

JAMES K. LOUTZENHISER

François TRUFFAUT

DAVID NICHOLLS

B.T. Batsford Ltd · London

First published 1993

© David Nicholls 1993

Typeset by Servis Filmsetting Ltd,
Manchester
and printed in Great Britain by
The Bath Press, Avon

Published by
B.T. Batsford Ltd
4 Fitzhardinge Street
London W1H 0AH

A catalogue record for this book is available
from the British Library

ISBN 0-7134-6694-4

Frontispiece: François Truffaut in the early 1960s, at about the time of *Shoot the Pianist*.

Contents

1

New Wave

In the course of a career that spanned some 25 years and 21 feature films François Truffaut became the most popular French film-maker of his day, known and admired in America, Britain and Japan as much, if not rather more than in his native country. Indeed, for Americans he was almost the personification of the French cinema.

According to Milos Forman, when he arrived in the United States from Czechoslovakia he found that for American movie buffs Truffaut *was* the French cinema, as Federico Fellini *was* the Italian cinema and Ingmar Bergman *was* the Scandinavian cinema. This was a gross misunderstanding in all three cases, and especially ironic with regard to Truffaut, given his almost complete lack of nationalist feeling and his vocal admiration for American cinema. Furthermore, he achieved this dubious status of cultural ambassador despite the apparently eclectic nature of his films, both in style and subject matter, and his refusal to follow trends or be

Federico Fellini's *La Dolce Vita*, controversial winner of the Palme d'Or at Cannes in 1960, the year after *Les 400 Coups*, was more than any other single film emblematic of the international New Wave, capturing the restlessness and disillusionment below the surface of newly affluent western Europe. In this scene a band of *paparazzi* (a word bequeathed to international language by Fellini's film) are hounding a woman whose husband has just killed their two children and then shot himself. Truffaut admired what he called Fellini's 'healthiness', his 'tranquil mastery and amused invention', and both directors made consistently inventive use of autobiographical elements in their films, but stylistically and thematically Truffaut was to follow a very different course from the Maestro.

fashionable. In an age when the self-consciously 'modern' or 'modernist' attracted most critical attention and influenced commercial film-making, sometimes for the better but equally often for the worse, Truffaut became more deliberately classical, even 'old-fashioned' in approach. To young Americans Truffaut represented an ideal, a model of freedom, culture and independence, especially after 1974 when his *Day For Night* won the Oscar for Best Foreign Film and became a sizeable box-office success. Reality was less rosy. Viewed from outside France his success seemed easy, but his career had its ups and downs, its periods of elation and depression, and it was only in the last few years of a life tragically cut short in 1984 at the age of 53 that he settled into a groove of consistent artistic and financial success with his last three films: *The Last Metro* (1980), *The Woman Next Door* (1981) and *Vivement Dimanche* (1983).

Part of Truffaut's problem lay in his name being indelibly associated with the so-called 'New Wave' in French cinema, which burst upon a supposedly moribund native film scene in 1958, the year of General de Gaulle's return to power. Enmities and false impressions created in the late 1950s and early 1960s proved long-lasting, and virtually every Truffaut film in the late 1960s and 1970s was greeted by hostile critics with cries of 'the New Wave is over', 'Truffaut the young iconoclast has gone stale', or similar such facile witticisms. A movement that apparently promised to change the cinematic world had done no such thing, and Truffaut, the standard bearer of revolt, had joined the establishment and become old hat. Having first come to notice as a very opinionated young critic attacking the 'false idols' of the French cinema, Truffaut himself became the target of critical fashion and the new idols of the day. Nor did Truffaut's refusal ever to disavow the New Wave, the importance he attached to fidelity in friendship and principle, and his capacity for rigorous self-criticism exactly help his cause. With the passage of time, however, we can place the New Wave in perspective, free from polemics or extravagant theories, and thereby assess Truffaut's life, personality and achievement in a reasonable fashion.

Truffaut during the filming of *The Woman Next Door* in 1981.

THE *NOUVELLE VAGUE* AND THE FIFTH REPUBLIC

The phrase *nouvelle vague*, probably first coined by Françoise Giroud in *L'Express* (though there are other contenders), always contained a fair amount of critical hype. As Claude Chabrol, a critical colleague of Truffaut turned director at the same time, remarked with typical acerbity: 'we were sold like a brand of soap powder'. According to Chabrol;

> Giroud . . . one of the most scathing opponents of Gaullism, made her political adversaries the gift of a great advertising slogan. For, let there be no mistake about this, if the press talked about us so much, it was because they wished to establish the equation: de Gaulle equals Renewal. In the cinema as in everything else. The general arrives, the Republic changes, France is reborn. Look at this flowering of talent. The intellect blossoms in the shadow of the cross of Lorraine. Make way for the young![1]

There is undoubtedly some justification for Chabrol's irony: the coincidence of the New Wave in cinema with political crisis leading to the establishment of the Fifth Republic was fortuitous for commentators. But nothing could have been further from the preoccupations of a basically non-political, even anti-political artist like Truffaut than a desire to impart Gaullist glory and grandeur to French cinema. The phrase 'New Wave' was, and has been ever since, a boon for publicists and the lazier sort of journalist, and New Waves in cinema, theatre, rock music and almost anything else have come thick and fast since 1958, coming to mean the rejection by one generation of the attitudes and style of its immediate predecessor. Giroud had unleashed a journalistic monster.

Beneath the hype and sloganizing, however, lay several interrelated realities: changes in the system of state support for the cinema, allowing first-time directors to make films more easily; the entry into film-making of a bunch of turbulent critics, including Truffaut and Chabrol, associated with the magazine *Cahiers du Cinéma*; technical changes, including the new lightweight Arriflex camera and new faster film stock, allowing more direct and improvisatory ways of filming on location, for example in bright sunlight; the rise of a new generation of male and female stars to replace the older 'sacred monsters' of French cinema; and the portrayal on film of new social and moral attitudes, especially about sex. From the technical point of view, the title of 'first New Wave feature film' should probably go to Agnès Varda's *La Pointe Courte* (1956), though Varda did not benefit from the unruly reputation of her male counterparts at the *Cahiers*, while Roger Vadim's *And God Created Woman* (1957), which launched the phenomenon of Brigitte Bardot, was the major breakthrough in its portrayal of a young woman who enjoyed sex for its own sake and flaunted her sexuality. (Strange as it may now seem, Vadim was considered a New Wave director until excluded from the brotherhood by Truffaut in 1961, when he replaced Truffaut's friend, Jean Aurel, as director of the Bardot vehicle *La Bride sur le Cou*, leading to a much publicized quarrel.) But not even Bardot could save a French film industry hit in the mid-1950s by falling box-office returns and hampered by a subsidy system based on advance on receipts that encouraged the kind of 'safe', expensive films that Truffaut the critic excoriated on aesthetic grounds. Vadim, one of only five new directors to appear in 1956, had spent many frustrating years as an assistant director before getting his chance. Changes in the aid laws in 1959, however, allowed aid to a first film on the basis of a submitted script, with the result that between 1958 and 1961 over 100 new directors made their first features. For quite a number of them it was also their last, but that was not the point: a wave of huge proportions did seem for a while to be sweeping all before it in the French cinema.

When Truffaut's first feature film, *Les 400 Coups*, won the director's prize at Cannes in 1959, one year after Truffaut the critic had been banned from the festival and replied in kind with articles such as 'Cannes, eleven years of political intrigues and publicity scandals', this was taken as a sign that the New Wave was triumphant and established Truffaut as its chief figure-head. In 1958 Chabrol's *Le Beau Serge* and Louis Malle's *Lift to the Scaffold* had been ignored by the official festival and shown unofficially in local cinemas; in 1959, thanks to Truffaut's film, a new generation of French cinema had been officially consecrated. Yet Truffaut's largely autobiographical portrait of a troubled early adolescence was very far from being a 'typical' New Wave film. Hostile or sceptical critics – and there were many – were disturbed by the apparent superficiality, the self-conscious avoidance of 'important issues' in most of the new 'youthful' films. The caricature of a New Wave film, created with only slight exaggeration by such observers, would feature the newly affluent 'modern' youth of France, enamoured of American cars and American cigarettes, freewheeling through the Latin Quarter or chic Mediterranean holiday spots in frantic and somewhat desperate pursuit of a good time. In part, this was the manifestation on celluloid of what Truffaut himself christened *le Saganisme*, after Françoise Sagan, author of *Bonjour Tristesse*, whose most affluent adepts gathered near Cannes at Saint-Tropez, thereby giving this once sleepy fishing village world-wide notoriety. It was also the French version of an international phenomenon, represented most vividly

Antoine Doinel in prison in *Les 400 Coups*, prior to being sent (as had Truffaut) to an Observation Centre for Juvenile Delinquents. Antoine throws away the disgusting coffee being handed him here and prefers to roll a cigarette with old newspaper. Though based on Truffaut's own experience, Antoine's misfortunes clearly struck a chord with the public: the film attracted more than 250,000 spectators during its first Paris run, helping to make it Truffaut's biggest financial success until *The Last Metro* 20 years later.

by Fellini's *La Dolce Vita* and in working-class costume by British Free Cinema, most notably by Albert Finney's hedonistic Arthur in *Saturday Night and Sunday Morning*. The west European cinema was reacting at last to the Age of Affluence, when young people had money in their pockets like never before. Yet nothing and nobody could have been further from Truffaut's preoccupations than the gilded youth who people the screens in, for example, Chabrol's *Les Cousins*, Jacques Doniol-Valcroze's *L'Eau à la Bouche* or Jacques Rozier's *Adieu Philippine*, the film seen by Truffaut and others as the epitome of the *nouvelle vague*.

COMMITMENT TO THE CINEMA

For all that, however, once the New Wave had been invented it had to be defended by those implicated in it. Both Truffaut and Chabrol later made this clear: to attack one New Wave film was by implication to attack them all, no matter how different they may have been one from another, and therefore all New Wave films, or those described as such, had to be defended against their detractors. The *Cahiers* group, including Truffaut, Chabrol and Doniol-Valcroze, as well as Jean-Luc Godard, Jacques Rivette and the somewhat older Eric Rohmer, were seen as the coherent hard core of the New Wave. Time was to show that they had very diverse artistic personalities, initially united only by commitment to the cinema as a means of personal expression, but up to 1964 at least, when the New Wave may be declared as being over, they were forced to stand together. Truffaut and Godard, who later fell out violently, praised each other's work in print and collaborated artistically and financially at the beginning of their two very different careers. The lasting legacy of the New Wave was in giving a number of talented, if often wayward individuals to French and world cinema. Truffaut himself never ceased to defend it and to help his comrades from the heroic days throughout the 1960s and (Godard excepted) the 1970s. Yet artistically he stood out from the beginning as untypical of the *nouvelle vague*, certainly as it was understood by hostile critics. He was never deliberately 'modern', preferring to quote Salvador Dali's advice to young painters: 'Don't worry about being modern, because unfortunately you will be, whatever you do.' Instead he liked to describe himself as a 'man of the 1930s and 1940s', profoundly marked by the cinema of his childhood during the Occupation, the silent cinema and the classical Hollywood cinema. His preoccupations were always far removed from the intellectual concerns of a Godard or a Rivette, being both more down-to-earth and more emotional. To discover the reasons for this we have to look first at his early life and his road to film-making.

2

A Life for the Movies

François Truffaut was born in Paris on 6 February 1932; his parents were married on 9 November 1933. Thus appears the greatest mystery in his life: was Roland Truffaut really his father? In *Les 400 Coups* it is revealed that the father of Antoine Doinel, Truffaut's *alter ego*, is really his stepfather, having married his mother when Antoine was a baby, while in the same film the English class at Antoine's school has to repeat over and again the phrase written on the blackboard: 'Where is the father?' This question runs through Truffaut's work: Adèle Hugo in *The Story of Adèle H* murmurs obsessively, 'I was born of an unknown father', while in *The Man Who Loved Women*, another partial self-portrait, the father is absent from the hero's childhood memories, there is only his mother with her dozens of lovers. If Truffaut or his closest friends ever really knew the truth, they never said. All we have are ambiguous remarks and the evidence of the films. Explaining his anti-nationalism Truffaut once said: 'I don't feel 100 per cent French and I don't know the full truth about my origins'.[1] It is probably best left at that, except that the question makes his later search for a spiritual father all the more poignant.

Truffaut spent his childhood on the lower slopes of Montmartre, in the neighbourhood below the place Pigalle. The family was comfortably off and *petit bourgeois*, neither rich nor poor. Roland Truffaut worked in an architect's office, while François's mother, Jeanine de Montferrand, was a secretary at the magazine *L'Illustration*. Both parents, however, were more interested in pursuing their hobby of *alpinisme*, taking off every Sunday to go walking in the forest of Fontainebleau, than they were in their son, who on such occasions was either dumped with relatives or left alone. Young François was not mistreated or deprived materially, he was ignored and thereby humiliated. His mother could not stand noise around the apartment, and François was not allowed to play there or in the street.

Like Bertrand Morane in *The Man Who Loved Women*, he took refuge in reading and became, not surprisingly, a rather withdrawn child, attending the local nursery school, but solitary and with few friends. Responsibility for looking after him was taken first by his maternal grandmother, Geneviève de Montferrand, with whom he seems to have got on well, but when she became too old, nobody in particular was responsible . He never forgave his mother for treating him as if he was an inconvenience visited upon her: if in his semi-autobiographical films the father is absent or ineffectual, the mother is neglectful and irresponsible.

His formal education was practically non-existent. He attended several schools, usually came bottom of the class, and later recalled the absurdities of school life under the Occupation, writing letters to and songs in praise of Marshal Pétain. Truffaut was for all practical purposes an autodidact, and his education was provided by books and films. He had two close friends who shared his passions. Robert Lachenay, who became in effect Antoine Doinel's friend René in *Les 400 Coups*, had an even more bizarre family background than Truffaut. His father, a one-time president of the Jockey Club of Paris, was a scion of the highest reaches of the Parisian *haute bourgeoisie*, but had gambled away most of his money, leaving the family in genteel poverty. Lachenay's mother, a former dancer at the Folies Bergères who thought she had made a good marriage, had become an alcoholic and was to die of liver failure at the age of 42. Luckily for the two youngsters, her permanent state of inebriation meant that she did not notice how much time they spent in the Lachenay residence, a vast apartment which was mostly empty because the furniture had had to be sold to make ends meet. It was here that François and Robert spent many hours they should have spent at school, and where François avoided going home – he once spent two weeks there. It was here also that the two boys stored their 'cinema archive': a vast collection of dossiers on individual films and directors, press cuttings and stills stolen from outside cinemas during nocturnal raids through Paris, as featured in the dream-memory of Ferrand, the director played by Truffaut in *Day For Night*.

A measure of stability was provided by the third member of the trio, Claude Thibaudat, later better known as Claude Vega, the actor and impressionist: he appears in *Bed and Board* as the mysterious 'strangler' who turns out to be a female impersonator and is seen 'doing' Delphine Seyrig on television. Thibaudat, though he joined the other two in clandestine visits to the cinema, was more settled, doing well at school and with a stable family life. Truffaut seems to have found warmth and understanding in Thibaudat's mother, who dubbed him 'my little Voltaire' because of the precocity of his reading, which, although it was the only thing which ever got him any good marks at school, he kept secret from his parents.

Truffaut was always somewhat vague about the precise dates of the important events of his childhood and adolescence, but his discovery of the cinema seems to have come in 1940. He remembered his first film vividly: Abel Gance's *Paradis Perdu*, with Fernand Gravey and 'the extraordinarily beautiful' Micheline Presle. In particular he noted the emotional reaction of the audience to this story of young men going off to fight in the First World War. For Truffaut it was love at first sight. In his eyes Gance was always a genius, and any actress in a Gance film was 'the greatest actress in the world'. Later, probably in 1942, he bunked off school to see Marcel Carné's *Les Visiteurs du Soir*. That evening his aunt called to take him to the cinema and had chosen *Les Visiteurs du Soir*. Unable to admit that he had seen it that very afternoon, he found himself seeing it twice in one day. Thus began his habit of seeing films over and over again, 'to enter more and more intimately into a work I admired until attaining the illusion of reliving its creation'. He saw Henri-Georges Clouzot's *Le Corbeau* so many times that he knew the dialogue by heart. This highly controversial film, banned after the Liberation, told the story of an epidemic of anonymous letters in a provincial town, and seemed to sum up what Truffaut saw around him: 'collaboration, informing, the black market, resourcefulness in surviving, and cynicism'.[2]

The cinema, therefore, as well as being a sensual pleasure for the eyes, ears and mind, became for Truffaut a handle on life. It could also be a way of giving shape to personal desires, unadmittable in real life. He confessed to having seen Sacha Guitry's *Le Roman d'un Tricheur* more than ten times and, following one particularly sharp family crisis, four times in one sitting. In Guitry's film a young boy, through sheer pig-headedness, refuses to eat the mushrooms served at dinner, with the result that his entire family dies poisoned and he alone survives. From that point on he decides to make trickery and deception the guide-lines for his life. One can easily see how this would have appealed to Truffaut, who came to know the dialogue by heart. This was also the beginning of his admiration for Guitry and his variety of amoral fable: indeed, the shadow of *Le Roman d'un Tricheur* may be detected behind *A Gorgeous Kid Like Me*.

TRUFFAUT THE ANTI-HERO

François, with or without Lachenay and Thibaudat as accomplices, would sneak into cinemas by the emergency exits or toilet windows and try to immerse himself in the film, sitting close to the screen in an attempt to enter into the action and identify with the characters. His anti-heroic attitude, created by what he saw around him, was strengthened. He was not keen on costume pictures, war films or westerns, going more for crime movies and love stories. 'Unlike most young spectators', he wrote later, 'I did not identify with heroic heroes but with weaker characters and more systematically with all those who found themselves in a state of guilt.'[3] Some of this was to remain in his adult make-up: his enthusiasm for Hitchcock becomes logical, and he never showed much interest in conventional male heroism. Cinema-going was illicit and dangerous, perpetually accompanied by the fear of getting caught. It was more than an education, it was a perilous adventure embarked upon by a shy and sensitive boy. In the years of the Occupation, when the streets of Pigalle were dark with something more than night, dominated by Corsican gangsters and illicit sex in shop doorways after curfew, and the family home was cold and unwelcoming, the cinema for Truffaut became something more than the escape it was for millions of French people. It was a refuge, though not a secure one, and already a source of creativity, a way of making sense of the world. The idea of clandestinity was to run through his work: there is a direct line from Antoine Doinel hiding from his family in Truffaut's first feature film to Julien Vercel, the hero of his last, *Vivement Dimanche*, hiding in the back of his office while his secretary tries to clear him of a murder charge and its attendant Hitchcockian guilt. The films of his childhood made a permanent impression: a cinema of studio-based stylization to which he paid tribute in *Day For Night* and *The Last Metro*, the expression of emotional truth through the artificial re-enactment of imaginary events.

The Liberation brought no new freedom to the now 14-year-old Truffaut. The years between 1945 and 1950 are the most obscure of his life. Even his voluminous correspondence is unreliable: he was economical with the truth even with his few close friends. One cannot blame him for this confusion. Moving away from home and sleeping where he could, he worked briefly in a succession of menial jobs, including stints as a stores assistant, a welder, and a night porter in a hotel, like Antoine Doinel in *Stolen Kisses*. At times he knew real poverty, experiencing at first hand what it was like not having enough to eat. But he also took to frequenting the ciné-clubs that flourished in post-war Paris. The Liberation may not have succeeded in putting sufficient food into peoples' mouths, but it did make available a rich cinematic diet. Five years of Hollywood production was released virtually all at once, while, with the native industry struggling to re-establish itself, French films of the 1930s were re-released *en masse*, allowing Truffaut to discover Jean Renoir and, in one memorable afternoon in 1946 at the ciné-club 'La Chambre Noire', Jean Vigo, whose *Zéro de Conduite*, banned since its first release, was to be an inspiration for *Les 400 Coups*.

Delphine Seyrig in *Stolen Kisses*, the second of Antoine Doinel's full-length adventures and one of Truffaut's most popular movies. The film plays humorously with the refined otherworldly image of an actress mainly known as the star of such highly intellectual movies as *Last Year in Marienbad* and *Muriel*. To Antoine Fabienne Tabard is 'not a woman but a vision', and she has to go to considerable lengths to prove she is a real woman made of flesh and blood. In *Bed and Board* Claude Vega imitates Seyrig as she appears in both *Marienbad* and *Stolen Kisses*: Antoine is understandably amazed.

It was in the ciné-clubs that Truffaut first met André Bazin, the spiritual father he had been searching for, who with his wife, Janine, provided him with an alternative family and for a while a safe home. Bazin, although only 27 years old in 1945, was already well-known as an organizer of ciné-clubs and film critic for several journals engendered by the Resistance and now emerged from obscurity, including the *Parisien Libéré* and the Communist controlled *L'Ecran Français*. Bazin's own intellectual background was in the centre-left Catholicism of the review *Esprit*, which in a secularized form may be seen in Truffaut's own mature moral outlook. For the moment, however, Truffaut was more interested in emulating Bazin by setting up, with Lachenay, his own ciné-club, with the 'pretentious but how revealing' name of 'Cercle Cinémane'. But their partner in the club turned out to be a swindler, and they could not show the advertised films. This adventure, the precise date of which is obscure, together with his continual running away from home, caused Roland Truffaut to drag François to the police and thence to the Observation Centre for Delinquent Minors at Villejuif. Here he encountered the depths of misery, the abandoned youth of the immediate post-war period, living on their wits, mostly by theft. This experience was to serve as the basis for the final section of *Les 400 Coups* and Truffaut's later work on behalf of abandoned and neglected children.

Bazin came to Truffaut's rescue, taking responsibility for him so that he could leave the Centre. One father had put François in prison, another got him out. He provided Truffaut with a home at Bry-sur-Marne on the outskirts of Paris and with a relatively congenial job as a projectionist with the organization Travail et Culture, his first work connected with the cinema. Travail et Culture was dedicated to 'taking culture to the masses' by staging plays and showing films in factories and other workplaces, and Bazin was one of the organizers. The work did not last long because the organization was taken over by the Communist Party and bourgeois deviationists like Bazin expelled, but it was while working for it that Truffaut met Alain Resnais and Chris Marker, among the future rejuvenators of French cinema.

At the same time, under Bazin's guidance and inspiration, he took his first steps into film criticism. Truffaut said of Bazin that he was less a film critic than a writer on film, more concerned to analyze and describe films than to judge them. This was an example he only half followed: Truffaut's criticism became violently judgemental of films he disliked; with those he liked, however, he took care to analyze how and why they worked. His very first article appeared in the *Bulletin du Ciné-Club du Quartier Latin* on the occasion of the re-release of Renoir's *La Règle du Jeu*, which had been banned during the Occupation, and gave a detailed description of the differences between the new version and that which had been shown before the war. He also succeeded in getting published in *Elle* and especially *La Gazette du Cinéma*, precursor of the famous *Cahiers*, where he met Jacques Doniol-Valcroze and Maurice Schérer, better known as Eric Rohmer. All this was under Bazin's tutelage. 'From the day when he found me my first work involved with the cinema', Truffaut later wrote, 'I became his adoptive son, and I owe to him everything good that happened in my life from then on. He taught me to write about the cinema, he corrected and published my first articles, and it was thanks to him that I was able to become a director'.[4]

In 1950, on a bizarre impulse following an incident when he had sold Lachenay's books to raise money and was afraid to confront his friend, Truffaut joined the army, anticipating his national service by three years and running the risk of being sent to Indo-China, where the French war against the Vietnamese nationalists was reaching its height. He asked to join the Army Cinematographic Service, but was in fact attached to an artillery regiment and sent to Germany for training. One result was that his hearing, with which he had always had problems, was permanently damaged: in *Day For Night*, playing the director Ferrand, he wears a hearing aid. He stuck it out well at first, but on leave in Paris before being sent to Indo-China he went AWOL – there were, after all, so many new films to be seen. He was arrested, escaped, recaptured, and sent to military prison in Germany as a deserter. Bazin had to come to his rescue once again, and Truffaut was eventually discharged for 'instability of character', like Antoine Doinel at the beginning of *Stolen Kisses*.

Even in his military prison Truffaut had been less worried about his own fate than that of Orson Welles's *Othello*, withdrawn from the Venice Film Festival in favour of Lawrence Olivier's *Hamlet*. In an interview in 1974 he admitted that

> there is no doubt that my love for the cinema had its neurotic side . . . I would hardly be exaggerating if I said that the cinema saved my life . . . If I threw myself into the cinema, this was probably because my life gave me no satisfaction during my childhood, that is to say the Occupation years. 1942 is an important date for me; that was when I began to see a lot of films. Between the ages of 10 and 19 I threw myself into films.[5]

This insatiable appetite was both sensual and educational: 'Everything I knew I learnt through films. My ideas on life pass through the cinema. One learns the history, the past and present of the cinema at the Cinémathèque . . . It is a permanent education. I am one of those people who need to see old films again and again, silent films and the first talkies.'[6]

For the young Truffaut the cinema was mistress and teacher, and the Cinémathèque Française was where she dwelt. Founded in 1948 by Henri Langlois, the Cinémathèque presented the classics of the cinema. The best known attracted huge audiences, the less known, films by Maurice Stiller or F.W. Murnau, had a small band of devotees, including Truffaut, Godard, Rivette and Suzanne Schiffman, a young Parisienne of the same age as Truffaut and destined to become his indispensable collaborator. Truffaut was the youngest and most disorderly of the band, always trying to get in without paying and flagrantly ignoring the 'No Smoking' signs. But here he learnt in haphazard fashion the entire history of the cinema, and was soon carried away by the proselytizing zeal of the autodidact, for the passionate youth was also an angry young man.

CRITICISM AND THE *CAHIERS DU CINÉMA*

In the world of criticism the *Cahiers du Cinéma*, run essentially by Bazin, Doniol-Valcroze, Schérer/Rohmer and Jean-Charles Tacchella, had taken over the reins of the now defunct *Gazette du Cinéma*. Truffaut started writing for the *Cahiers* in 1953 and became the most intransigent and violently opinionated of its critics, giving the journal its identity and combative reputation. At the same time, thanks to Jean Aurel, another future collaborator, he continued his battles in the weekly *Arts*, the new owner of which, Jacques Laurent, took a malicious delight in the scandals caused by the young critic. Truffaut learned to write as he wrote, getting his opinions into focus by setting them out in print and arguing and debating with Bazin and with Chabrol, Godard and company. One expects, therefore, more passion than controlled consistency in his writings, but what gave his criticism its intransigence was its directness. Whereas Godard, for example, could scale the heights of poetic incomprehensibility with ease, and Chabrol and Rohmer evinced the anguish of the Catholic intellectual, Truffaut said what he thought in straightforward fashion and without mincing his words. The result was eminently readable, often very perceptive, sometimes downright silly, almost always overstated, and clearly the work of someone who expected a lot from the cinema and was liable to explode with anger at those films which failed to deliver. But, as with all the critics on the *Cahiers*, the hidden agenda of Truffaut's criticism is his own future film-making. In criticizing the work of others he was defining, if only semi-consciously, the kind of films he himself wanted to make.

Truffaut became notorious for his attacks on the currently dominant and most lauded forms of film-making in France, what he called in a famous article of 1953 'a certain tendency in French cinema'.[7] What annoyed him most were, on the one hand, the kind of elaborately filmed but simplified literary adaptations that gave audiences the impression they had 'seen' the work of Stendhal, Raymond Radiguet or whoever, but which were to Truffaut's mind betrayals of the authors concerned, and on the other hand, self-consciously 'important' social dramas, which, under a thin veneer of nonconformity, in fact flattered audiences into believing how intelligent and 'concerned' they were. His attacks on the makers of these films, including the directors Jean Delannoy, André Cayatte and Claude Autant-Lara, and the screenwriters Jean Aurenche and Pierre Bost, were often viciously personal. 'The French cinema', he said in the title of a notorious article in *Arts*, 'is collapsing under the weight of false legends.'[8] This created ill-feeling, which in Autant-Lara's case lasted throughout Truffaut's life and beyond. Yet Truffaut's inherent generosity, hidden for the moment by the opinionated dogmatism of youth, still broke through. When Autant-Lara made a film that Truffaut liked, such as *La Traversée de Paris* (1956) or *En Cas de Malheur* (1958), he praised it, even if rather grudgingly. For even in his most violent polemics Truffaut was stating and developing a moral viewpoint about the cinema, which he would later put into practice.

The basis of criticism in the *Cahiers*, largely created by Truffaut, was the so-called *politique des auteurs*, a policy – and *not*, whatever it may have become later, a 'theory' – that favoured those films which expressed the personality of their directors or *auteurs*. Quite simply, a film was to be valued to the extent to which it reflected the personality of its maker. Making a film may be a collective endeavour, and Hollywood a factory turning out cinematic product, but the ultimate responsibility for any film lies with its director, and it his duty to remain true to the film, the audience, and therefore himself. There are no bad films, only mediocre directors. The flood of discussion sparked off by the *politique des auteurs* has tended to ignore the fact that for Truffaut at least it was fundamentally a moral outlook, based on what he saw as the responsibility of the director in bringing a subject to the screen. His viewpoint is that of a film buff and future director head over heels in love with his chosen means of expression. 'The film of tomorrow', he wrote, 'will not be directed by functionaries of the camera but by artists for whom the making of a film is a tremendous and exhilarating adventure. The film of tomorrow will be in the image of he who has made it. . . . The film of tomorrow will be an act of love.'[9] Love and passion for the cinema is what Truffaut wanted to see up on the screen, and this is what his favourite directors had in common.

Taken to extremes, of course, the *politique des auteurs* becomes absurd. Logically, one did not need to see a film to know how good it was, just know who directed it. 'Don't you understand', Truffaut recalled shouting at Bazin, 'that the worst film by Howard Hawks is better than the best film by John Huston!' So *Land of the Pharoahs* is a better film than *The Maltese Falcon*! He later amended his opinion to 'the worst film by Howard Hawks is *more interesting* than the best film by John Huston', but this is not much help. Truffaut did not like Huston, but he did like *The Maltese Falcon*, therefore responsibility for *The Maltese Falcon* must lie elsewhere – with Humphrey Bogart, perhaps. Huston's gift, if he had one, lay in spotting talent, though as everyone knows he had first wanted George Raft for the role of Sam Spade. But, for all its occasional absurdity and the intellectual tangles it produced, the *auteur* policy was crucial for Truffaut and the other *Cahiers* critics in strengthening their faith in the cinema as a means of personal expression and providing them with models to emulate. The ideological content of that expression was less important than its being authentic. So Truffaut praised equally the anarchist Jean Vigo and the Catholic Robert Bresson because they both made films that could not have been made by anyone else, and the same goes for Charlie Chaplin and Ingmar Bergman, Frank Capra and Luis Buñuel, Nicholas Ray and Max Ophuls, and, above and beyond all the rest, Jean Renoir and Alfred Hitchcock.

The greatest strength of the *auteur* policy was that it replaced one hierarchy of judgement based on the 'cinema of quality' and the fallacy of impressive content, with another based on the morality of personal expression, which, though obviously debatable, was also more open and democratic, based on talent rather than prestige. The *Cahiers* critics were renowned for their praise of Hollywood directors, with Hitchcock and Howard Hawks at the summit, so that they became known as the 'Hitchcocko-Hawksians'. But Truffaut's criticism went beyond this in abolishing all distinction between 'commercial' and 'art' cinema, the 'popular' and the 'prestigious'. Reviewing his criticism in retrospect, he was proud that he had been neither a snob nor an inverted snob, 'seeing no differences in kind between films, only differences in degree'. All films were commercial objects in that they were subject to buying and selling, and this was just as important for an 'art house' director as for one immersed in the Hollywood system. As an illustration of his attitude he cited the example of Hitchcock's *Psycho* and Bergman's *The Virgin Spring*, both released in the same year to completely opposite reactions from the critics. Whereas Hitchcock was lambasted for making a 'sick' and trivial film, Bergman was praised to the skies and awarded the Oscar for Best Foreign Film. For Truffaut, however, these were two films on essentially the same subject, versions of 'Little Red Riding Hood'. Both films were equally valid because 'through these two films, Bergman and

Hitchcock admirably expressed and liberated a part of the violence within themselves'.[10] To other viewers this may not seem to be the real significance of either *Psycho* or *The Virgin Spring*, but Truffaut's main point is well taken: Hitchcock and Bergman are both great film directors.

Truffaut's tastes were wide-ranging. Wherever he could detect an authentic authorial voice at work his praises resounded. He admired the acknowledged greats, such as Gance, Chaplin or Welles; Hollywood free spirits, such as Robert Aldrich, Billy Wilder, Samuel Fuller or Nicholas Ray; congenially independent Frenchmen, such as Jacques Becker, Jean Cocteau, Alexandre Astruc or Jacques Tati; 'outsiders' such as Bergman, Ophuls, Buñuel, Fellini or Roberto Rossellini; or his fellow New Wavers, such as Chabrol, Godard, Resnais or Louis Malle. But it was probably his dislikes which, by a process of reaction, had the greatest influence in determining what kind of films he himself would go on to make. He reserved his greatest spleen for what he called 'bluffer's cinema', not only the French 'cinema of quality', but also his particular *bêtes noires*, John Huston and David Lean.

If Truffaut exercised and exorcized the arrogance of youth in his often immature criticism, in his films he never claims to be the sole possessor of 'the Truth' about anything. He saw the presentation of a clear-cut and easily understood 'moral' in a film as a way of despising the audience, and he himself despised the audiences who went along with it – the people he called in French terms 'the Champs Elysées audience', who had no real interest in the cinema but used it as a quick cultural fix, or something to talk about at dinner parties. These were the well-heeled spectators who could pride themselves on spotting the moral of a Huston or Lean film and then happily ignore it in their everyday lives, especially if it was about money, as in Huston's *The Treasure of the Sierra Madre*. Reviewing Alexandre Astruc's *Les Mauvaises Rencontres* in 1955 Truffaut related an exchange between Astruc and a journalist at the Venice Film Festival. 'You have overestimated the audience,' said the journalist. 'One can never overestimate the audience', replied Astruc.[11] This became Truffaut's attitude. He certainly wanted to please his audience, but not by patronizing or flattering them. Truffaut preferred to appeal to an audience's intelligence. Sometimes he succeeded, sometimes he failed, but probably only in about the same proportions as the marketing experts of Hollywood.

Truffaut had another gripe against Huston. Having read Lillian Hellman's account of the making of *The Red Badge of Courage*, he was disgusted by the way in which Huston, once it was clear that the film was not going to work, walked away, leaving the editors to salvage what they could on the cutting table. This was, in Truffaut's eyes, an abdication of moral responsibility. The director should be totally committed to his film, make it to the best of his ability, and see it through to the end, not shrug off responsibility when the going got tough. Film-making was too important ever to walk away from. This is the attitude he gives to Joëlle, the script girl played by Nathalie Baye in *Day For Night*, when he has her say that she would leave a man for a film, but never a film for a man.

But in reality his distaste for and misunderstanding of Huston and Lean was also a rationalization of his anti-heroic stance. The questions raised, for example, in the Lean–Robert Bolt collaborations *The Bridge on the River Kwai* (the enormous success of which in France Truffaut seemed to take as a personal insult) and *Lawrence of Arabia* about the nature of heroism and the psychological make-up of the hero, were of no interest to Truffaut. He remained too much the child of the Occupation, forced to write laudatory letters to Marshal Pétain, with an extra vitamin biscuit as reward for the best. His interest was not in war heroes, but in the ordinary people who had to struggle through and survive wartime conditions, the people portrayed in *The Last Metro*. Truffaut's heroes were writers and film-makers, those who gave the best of themselves in artistic creation, not in politics or warfare, and who were heroes despite themselves, without wanting to be and above all without seeking to be.

If clandestine cinema-going and secret reading had been Truffaut's education, then writing film criticism was his higher education. Time and again in his reviews he refers to the 'lessons' to be drawn from a particular film or director. Even after he himself had become a director loaded with acclaim this attitude did not change. Reviewing Samuel Fuller's *Verboten* in 1960 he wrote: 'I shall go and see this film again and again, because I always come out of a Samuel Fuller film admiring and jealous, because I like to receive lessons in cinema.'[12] Truffaut learned while writing, absorbing lessons in humanism from Renoir, effectiveness from Hitchcock, intelligence from Hawks, humility from Rossellini, and so on. Thus he disciplined his instincts by analysis: his review of Aldrich's *Vera Cruz*, for example, is mostly devoted to a breakdown of the screenplay, because this provides 'a dazzling lesson in how to construct a story'.[13]

His dislikes, on the other hand, were less disciplined and often too categorical and too violently expressed. In someone destined to remain nothing but a critic they would be unforgivable, but for someone whose ultimate goal was to make his own films they were a necessary evil, the indispensable process of rejection preceding an effort at construction. The unfortunate thing was that because Truffaut's conception of the cinema was based around the personalities of directors, his dislikes were too personalized and liable to be reciprocated in kind. Bazin, who quite rightly admired some of the directors attacked by Truffaut, at first hesitated about publishing his more intemperate outbursts in the *Cahiers*, but he probably realized that this was part of his protégé's growing up and that his inherent generosity and humanism would emerge in his own films and in his behaviour once he was in a position to help other people. This faith would be vindicated, but tragically Bazin did not live to see it.

Once he became a director himself Truffaut stopped criticizing his fellow film-makers. He never stopped writing about the cinema, but only in order to praise directors and films he admired. Talking with Julien Duvivier just before the older director's death, Truffaut tried to get him to admit that he had had a good career, 'varied and complete', and that taking everything into account it had been a good life and he should be proud of his achievements. Duvivier finally replied: 'Yes, I would feel happy . . . if it hadn't been for the critics.' This heartfelt declaration shocked Truffaut, who had in his time criticized Duvivier but who had just made his first feature. He told Duvivier that when as a critic he had insulted the French 'quality' film-makers, 'I had always been aware, deep down inside, that I was in the position of a policeman directing traffic in front of the Paris Opera while the bombs were falling on Verdun.'[14] This rather extravagant metaphor expresses Truffaut's view that presenting a film to the public represented a baptism of fire, each and every time one did it. The younger Truffaut had possibly not had the imagination to realize this, but Truffaut the director, naturally modest and somewhat shy, became only too well aware of it.

Journalism, however, was not Truffaut's only education. We cannot be certain when the *Cahiers* band decided that they would make their own films or who made his mind up first. Rohmer was already making shorts, but among the younger critics it was probably Rivette who decided first and persuaded the others. Their first effort was *Une Visite* in 1954, a silent short lasting 7 minutes 40 seconds and shot in Doniol-Valcroze's apartment, his wife only agreeing to this domestic disruption if the apprentice geniuses agreed to look after the couple's young daughter, Florence, who thereby gained a starring role and became the first child actor in a Truffaut film. Truffaut wrote and directed this slight anecdote, with Rivette behind the camera, Lachenay as 'assistant director and producer', and Resnais editing. Unreleased at the time, *Une Visite* was disinterred in 1982, much to the embarassment of all concerned, when Truffaut decided to place a copy in the archives of Les Films du Carrosse as part of his effort to secure the rights to all his work. It was, said Truffaut then, the work of an amateur and, what was worse, an amateur who tried to experiment. It is only of interest as a declaration of intent by Truffaut and the others.

More valuable for Truffaut were the two years he spent, on and off, as an assistant to Roberto Rossellini. During this period, between 1955 and 1957, Rossellini was out of favour with producers, the films he had made with Ingrid Bergman having flopped at the box office. Nor did he succeed in making a film during Truffaut's time with him, an experience which was invaluable in giving the young critic an insider's view of the difficulties involved in getting projects off the ground. Rossellini, he said later, cured him of his 'open-mouthed admiration' for Hollywood films, but it was the Italian's intransigent sticking to principle and refusal to compromise which acted as an example to the aspirant director. For example, one of the tasks performed by Truffaut for Rossellini was to prepare a treatment of *Carmen* based on Prosper Mérimée's original story. When all was ready the prospective producer insisted on casting Marina Vlady – a Hungarian blonde! – in the title role, and Rossellini dropped the project. The experience with Rossellini seems to have convinced Truffaut that the only way to make personal films would be to set up his own production company. He duly formed Les Films du Carrosse, named after Renoir's *Le Carrosse d'Or* (*The Golden Coach*), for his first real short film, *Les Mistons*.

Meanwhile Truffaut had married Madeleine Morgenstern, daughter of the producer Ignace Morgenstern, on 29 October 1957, with Bazin and Rossellini as witnesses. Two daughters, Laura, born in 1959, and Eva, born in 1961, were to result from this marriage. Haunted by his own loveless childhood, Truffaut endeavoured to be a good father. The girls remember him as more playmate than patriarch. Sundays were always set aside for them, and if he was forced to work the girls would be taken along: Eva recalls being taken to see the rushes of *Stolen Kisses* because they had to be viewed on a Sunday. He only turned heavy when his daughters appeared in his films. Eva, who played one of the group of children at the centre of *Small Change*, recalls her reluctance to kiss a boy she did not like: 'I said to my father: "I can't do it, I can't do it", and he said to me: "Listen, you are an actress, yes or no?" . . . The film took priority over personal feelings.'[15] Laura and Eva both appeared briefly in *The Wild Child*, along with Suzanne Schiffman's sons, Mathieu and Guillaume, and again in *Les Deux Anglaises* and *Small Change*, in which Laura is christened Madeleine Doinel, an amalgam of her mother's name and that of her father's *alter ego*. Unlike the younger Schiffmans, however, neither has pursued a career in the cinema.

The marriage with Madeleine only lasted four years, although she and Truffaut remained the best of friends thereafter. Truffaut, said Liliane David, later Liliane Dreyfus, 'was the kind of man you never left entirely'. Truffaut's relationship with Liliane, with whom he had been having an affair even while married to Madeleine, was broken up by Godard, whose own relationships with women were at this time extremely difficult. Truffaut seemed at the time to have forgiven his friend, but his underlying bitterness resurfaced when their friendship collapsed into rancour years later. Truffaut's private life after his marriage was complicated to say the least, and the details are both obscure and of no great importance. If we wish to know what he thought of Jeanne Moreau, the evidence is *Jules et Jim*; for Catherine Deneuve, it is *The Last Metro*; for Jacqueline Bisset, *Day For Night*; for Fanny Ardant, *The Woman Next Door* and *Vivement Dimanche*, and so on. A succession of women, mostly actresses, were lovers for a while, confidantes for life. The only one he lived with for any length of time was Deneuve, and this ended badly in 1971 with Truffaut's only nervous breakdown – a depression he forced himself out of by writing *Les Deux Anglaises*.

On the one hand, Truffaut loved women and valued their friendship and confidence; on the other hand, he clearly had a horror of settling down and forming a conventional couple. His timidity, sensitivity and fidelity in friendship appealed strongly to women. He could be somewhat annoying, impossible to get rid of, but also extraordinarily generous. For example, one of his last affairs was with Marie de Poncheville, who appears briefly in *The Green Room* under the name of Marie Jaoul. She was introduced to Truffaut by Marie-France Pisier, who was amused by her being almost exactly the real-life equivalent of the character played by Brigitte Fossey in *The Man Who Loved Women*, a publisher's assistant with ambitions to have her own publishing house. Marie eventually put an end to their affair by marrying a man she had met while on holiday in California and had known for only two weeks: this extreme measure was the only way to do it. But both during and after their affair Truffaut helped her, both morally and financially, to set up the publishing house Cinq Continents, which published his correspondence after his death. She has since, almost inevitably, become a film director under the name of Marie Jaoul de Poncheville.

Just before his death Truffaut had a third daughter, Jacqueline, with Fanny Ardant. But his films were also made in praise of women he did not have affairs with, like Bernadette Lafont, Claude Jade or Marie-France Pisier, all of whom he helped in their careers and were valued friends and collaborators. He was, quite simply, a man who loved women: real women and not stereotypes. In the world of the cinema, full of remarkable and talented women, a conventional private life was clearly an impossibility for a man like François Truffaut.

THE FIRST FILMS – *LES MISTONS* AND *LES 400 COUPS*

The troubles of the 'impossible couple' would figure largely in his later films, but first Truffaut's natural affinity with children, which obviously helped in the potentially tricky relationship with his daughters, appeared fully on screen in *Les Mistons*, released in 1958. If any artist's work is all contained, at least in embryo, in his or her first offering, then most of Truffaut's themes and obsessions are in *Les Mistons*: children, women, love and passion, the cinema, books, memory, death. Adapted from a short story by Maurice Pons, the film portrays the nascent sexual feelings of a gang of young adolescents in Nîmes, obsessed by and pestering Bernadette Lafont, whose lover, played by Gérard Blain, is eventually killed in a mountaineering accident. The cinematic references are breathtakingly impudent: recreations of two films by the Lumière brothers, *L'Arroseur Arrosé* and *Train Entering the Station at La Ciotat*. The cinema has been invented once, these references seem to imply; now I, François Truffaut, am inventing it again. Be that as it may, *Les Mistons* was well received, winning awards in Belgium, Germany and the United States. Its clumsy freshness is undoubtedly charming, showing the director as someone who knows about film, but is prepared to break the rules if necessity or inclination demand.

In making *Les Mistons* Truffaut discovered how much he enjoyed working with children. The boys were all recruited on the spot in Nîmes, according to the principles Truffaut later applied to his other films with children. *Les Mistons* announced his arrival behind the camera, showed that he was not all talk, gave him confidence, and sealed his friendships with Bernadette Lafont, with whom he was to work again on *A Gorgeous Kid Like Me*, and with Claude de Givray who was recruited to work on the film in a vague capacity simply because he owned a car in which the band could travel from Paris to Nîmes.

Les Mistons was distributed as support to Chabrol's *Le Beau Serge* by Pierre Braunberger's Les Films de la Pléiade. Braunberger, who had produced some of the great French classics of the 1930s, was one of the few producers astute enough to see the potential of the New Wave and produced several of its most significant films, including Godard's first feature, *A Bout de Souffle*. It was for Braunberger that Truffaut and Godard cobbled together *Une Histoire d'Eau*, making use of footage of floods in the Paris basin, to which was attached a slim anecdote involving Caroline Dim and Jean-Claude Brialy, another member of the band around the *Cahiers* and destined to become one of the most versatile actors of the New Wave. As a film it is frankly not very interesting, though the commentary written by Godard is typical in its mixture of extreme erudition and throwaway humour. For both directors the time had come to make a feature film, and in November 1958 Truffaut started shooting *Les 400 Coups*.

Truffaut's first feature seems to have become more autobiographical between conception and filming. Originally it was to have been *La Fugue d'Antoine*, one of a series of shorts about childhood of which *Les Mistons* was the first. But Truffaut and his co-scenarist Marcel Moussy, who had written a drama-documentary about delinquent youth for television, decided to turn the sketch into a full-length film. This was to have been about two children, a boy and a girl, both equally important. The girl, however, was eliminated: she was to re-appear 25 years later as *La Petite Voleuse*, which was to have been Truffaut's next film at the time of his death and was eventually directed by Claude Miller. As it was, Truffaut gave much of his own childhood experience to Antoine Doinel, helped by Moussy who advised him about what to include and what to leave out in constructing an acceptable fiction. Antoine thus became an amalgam of Truffaut and Jean-Pierre Léaud, the young actor chosen to play him. Pierre Braunberger, meanwhile, made a rare mistake in refusing to produce *Les 400 Coups*, so Truffaut's father-in-law, Ignace Morgenstern, stepped into the breach. Morgenstern's second-in-command, Marcel Berbert, joined Les Films du Carrosse, where he was to hold the financial reins through thick and thin for the rest of Truffaut's career, and was credited as Executive Producer on most of his films. Philippe de Broca, a member of the band with more experience of the film industry than most, was first assistant director, thereby avoiding any possible union troubles, while the splendid Henri Decae was director of photography. The Carrosse was ready to roll fully loaded for the first time.

Childhood behind bars. A publicity still for *Les 400 Coups* showing Antoine Doinel (Jean-Pierre Léaud) in the cage at the police station after his father has hauled him there for stealing a typewriter, one of several episodes in the film directly inspired by Truffaut's own childhood experience, and the most dramatic because it marks Antoine's definitive estrangement from the conventional world of family and school. The film blends Truffaut's experiences with the contribution of Marcel Moussy, a writer who had worked on television programmes dealing with familial and social problems.

The filming of *Les 400 Coups* got off to the worst possible start when André Bazin died, after a long struggle against illness, on 11 November 1958. But this seems to have acted as a spur to Truffaut: he had to make his film a success for Bazin's sake. As a debt of honour, the film is dedicated to Bazin's memory. The result was an unmitigated triumph. Antoine Doinel, the child of a loveless marriage, bunks off school to go to the cinema, spends nights out and steals the morning milk, hides out in a friend's apartment, steals his stepfather's typewriter, and is dumped in an Observation Centre for Delinquents: Truffaut settles his accounts with his childhood through the creation of a film. A good example of his creative use of his own past occurs when Antoine, who has been playing truant as usual, is asked why he has no note from his mother to explain his absence from school and blurts out: 'Because she's dead!' Sympathy all round. Until, that is, his mother turns up at the school. In real life this incident had involved Truffaut's uncle, who was associated with the Resistance. When asked why he had no note from him, Truffaut had said: 'Because he's been arrested by the Gestapo!' This lie had resulted in painful consequences for François. The real incident is thus updated and heightened for dramatic effect. In similar fashion, Antoine seeks comfort and joy in reading, just as Truffaut had done, but instead of merely admiring Balzac, he builds a shrine to him, complete with candles, and starts a fire in his parents' cramped apartment. Later he tries to pass off a passage from Balzac as his own work for an essay and is humiliated in front of his classmates as a result. Antoine thus becomes a version of François crossed with Léaud, and therefore less shy, more impulsive – and autobiography becomes fiction.

Despite the inherent gloom and anger of the subject matter, *Les 400 Coups* is the opposite of depressing. Truffaut succeeds in communicating what he had always looked for in films – the pleasure and privilege of film-making – and this, combined with his ability to look at childhood from the child's point of view, created a film which was not only a personal vindication but also a triumph of New Wave style over the 'cinema of quality'. The danger, as swiftly became apparent in other New Wave films, was that in breaking one set of conventions new ones were created. But Truffaut never broke rules just for the sake of it: the examples of the master directors were always in his mind, and he wanted to recapture the freedom in story-telling of the silent cinema and to place cinematic style at the service of story, characters and actors. Thus, while most of *Les 400 Coups* is tightly scripted, for the scene where Antoine is interrogated at the Detention Centre Truffaut himself posed questions to Léaud, allowed the boy to give his own answers, and then eliminated the questions, dissolving from one answer to the next. This is not strictly speaking improvisation or *cinéma vérité* (the now forgotten form of 'direct cinema', which Truffaut detested), but it does have a fresh, improvisatory look to it, and presents Antoine to us without imposing any judgement about him. The famous ending, a long tracking shot of Antoine running towards the sea to freedom (but what freedom?) and ending on a freeze frame of Antoine staring straight into camera, was also arrived at during filming as the only way to end the film. It was a device destined to become a cliché: Antoine faces us, making us feel guilty if we wish, but also free to project our own meanings onto his face. In context it is perfect, but Truffaut never used it again: that would have been too easy.

Doniol-Valcroze said of *Les 400 Coups* that making the film reconciled Truffaut to life in somewhat the same way that reaching the sea reconciles Antoine to life. Almost overnight the annoying and opinionated critic became a famous director, celebrated throughout the world. The triumph at Cannes must have tasted especially sweet. In 1958 Truffaut had been banned from the festival for writing that members of the jury had slept through showings of films; in 1959 he returned, accompanied by his New Wave colleagues, to receive the prize as best director. Shepherded through the social whirl by Jean Cocteau, who was used to that milieu, Truffaut and Léaud accepted the plaudits of the cinematic world. Three years later the poacher turned gamekeeper with a vengeance when Truffaut became president of the jury, which was a big mistake. Having denounced the political corruption and compromise of the festival, he now became a party to it. The Palme d'Or for 1962 went to a now forgotten Brazilian film, purely in order to encourage Latin American participation in the competition. It was to be the first and last time that Truffaut accepted such a post.

Apart from Cannes, *Les 400 Coups* won numerous other awards on both sides of the Atlantic and received an Oscar nomination for Best Original Screenplay. The selling of the film marks the beginning of Truffaut's connection with America. The publicity trip to the US, however, was not an altogether happy experience for Truffaut as he was shuttled from city to city, as yet unable to speak a word of English. Fortunately he was in the capable hands of Helen Scott, then head of public relations at the French Film Office in New York, and the friendship thus created was to last to the end of Truffaut's life. She became Truffaut's eyes and ears in New York, and later in Paris a trusted friend, and was to act as interpreter in his conversations with Hitchcock which became the famous 'Hitchcock/Truffaut' book.

The American rights of *Les 400 Coups* were sold for the very handy sum of half a million dollars. Truffaut immediately gave part of this money to Cocteau, who was having difficulty in completing his *Le Testament d'Orphée*, in which Léaud also made a brief appearance. Truffaut had managed to take advantage of the rise in the price of French films in America, caused essentially by Brigitte Bardot, and established his reputation permanently across the Atlantic. Throughout the 1960s American money was to be vital for Les Films du Carrosse. Whereas French producers were reluctant to put money into independent productions over which they had no control, American companies which had money tied up in Europe and which they were not allowed to 'repatriate', knew that for a relatively small investment they would get a product which stood a good chance of being profitable in America. Several of Truffaut's films were better received both by the critics and the art-house and campus publics in the US than in France. *The Story of Adèle H*, for example, which was a complete flop in France, was very successful in America, where it was distributed by Roger Corman.

All Truffaut's feature films, except *Shoot the Pianist* and *Fahrenheit 451*, were produced by Les Films du Carrosse. Except for the very cheapest films, these were made in association with a French co-producer/distributor, and with money from American distributors. More expensive films had aid from an Italian co-producer as well. Pierre Braunberger tried to make up for missing out on *Les 400 Coups* by producing *Shoot the Pianist*, Truffaut's second feature, but it was not nearly as profitable as the first. Thereafter, apart from the English adventure of *Fahrenheit 451*, Truffaut's fortunes were essentially those of his Carrosse. The Carrosse's journey was far from being a smooth one, though Truffaut never let financial problems disturb the family atmosphere of the company. With Marcel Berbert controlling the financial side of production, the Carrosse managed to stay on the road for the next 25 years.

THE EARLY 1960S – *SHOOT THE PIANIST*, *JULES ET JIM* AND THE ADVENTURES OF ANTOINE DOINEL

All Truffaut's films, except *Silken Skin* and *The Woman Next Door*, were long-term projects with in some cases a very long gestation period. Years could pass between the various stages of having the idea for a film, writing a script, deciding that the time was right to make it, and finding the financial backing. Truffaut's only consistent principle was that each film should be as big a contrast as possible with the preceding one. He certainly repeated himself, but never immediately, and most often left a period of seven or eight years between comparable projects. Applying this principle from the outset, for his second feature, again working with Marcel Moussy, he adapted David Goodis's novel *Down There* under its French title of *Tirez sur le Pianiste*. Released in November 1960 at a time when New Wave films were coming thick and fast, it was not a financial success, baffling audiences expecting a 'normal' gangster picture. Some critics in France and America liked it, however, and it has always proved popular when revived in art houses.

The *Pianist*, like Godard's *A Bout de Souffle*, is a homage to the American B picture, the kind of small-scale Hollywood product in which, so the *Cahiers* critics believed, the personality of an *auteur* could express itself more readily then in large-scale 'prestige' projects. Goodis was one of those American pulp writers, like Cornell Woolrych or Jim Thompson, who were always more appreciated in France than at home. Kept in print by Gallimard's 'Série Noire', they were the favourite reading of intellectuals as well as the mass public. Truffaut and Moussy stuck fairly closely to the novel, but changed the nature of the hero to fit the personality of Charles Aznavour. The result is great fun, like a *film noir* redesigned by a slightly crazy comic-book artist complete with little inserts, as when a gangster swears on his mother's head, 'may she die if I'm lying', and the camera cuts to an old lady falling backwards out of her chair. Aznavour gives his best ever film performance as a typical Truffaut hero, timid and secretive, needing the help of women. He is supported by Truffaut's discovery Marie Dubois. Her real name was Claudine Huzé, but she was rebaptised with the name of the heroine of a novel by Jacques Audiberti, one of Truffaut's favourite authors, who was 'the poet of the divine mystery of women' and original poser of the Truffaldian question: 'Are women magic?'.

The *Pianist* taught Truffaut several things and established his future working methods. It is a gangster picture, but Truffaut found that he could not take gangsters seriously. The pair of kidnappers become comical figures, like children playing at being gangsters – Truffaut was incapable of putting conventional heavies on screen. But the Carrosse team was coming together: Lachenay was still involved as Truffaut's right hand man, but more important were Raoul Coutard, director of photography in chief to the New Wave; Georges Delerue for the music, to whom Truffaut left total freedom; and especially Suzanne Schiffman, officially script-girl, but more important than that as Truffaut's most long-lasting collaborator.

Truffaut did not allow the semi-failure of the *Pianist* to overturn the Carrosse. In 1962 he produced *Tire au Flanc*, a remake of a Renoir silent directed by Claude de Givray. In the film Truffaut appears briefly as a soldier in prison reading Goethe (all Truffaut's life is on film somewhere!). For his own next feature, going for contrast once again, he turned to something he had originally considered for his debut: an adaptation of Henri-Pierre Roché's *Jules et Jim*.

Truffaut had discovered this first, autobiographical novel by the 76-year-old Roché by chance in 1955 and immediately made contact with the author. Roché, whose work had been little noticed by critics or the public, was flattered and delighted by Truffaut's attention, and the two remained in contact until the author's death in April 1959. Roché notably approved the choice of Jeanne Moreau to play his heroine Kathe, renamed Catherine in the film. Truffaut had first met Moreau when Jean-Claude Brialy had brought her along to watch the filming of *Les 400 Coups* and both had ended up making brief guest appearances. At that moment, apparently, Truffaut had decided that she would be his Catherine, the incarnation of womanhood, pursued, loved but never dominated by Jules and Jim.

Jules et Jim, filmed in Paris and on the Côte d'Azur between April and June 1961 and released in January 1962, was a huge success. One might be tempted to call it Truffaut's masterpiece, if the very word 'masterpiece' had not been enough to make him collapse with laughter. Truffaut wrote the screenplay with Jean Gruault, while Schiffman, Coutard, Delerue and Berbert were all on board. Truffaut's love and admiration for Moreau is evident whenever she is on screen; the German, Jules, is the experienced Oskar Werner, while the Frenchman, Jim, is Henri Serre, making his film debut and chosen because of his resemblance to the young Roché. Marie Dubois appears again, while Boris Bassiak (Serge Rezvani) and his wife Danielle contributed their acting talents, their house as a location, and the song 'Le Tourbillon', sung by Moreau and expressing 'the whirlwind of life' successfully captured by the film. Truffaut employs the wide screen black-and-white format superbly, using every trick in the book – ellipses, irises, partial black-out of the screen – but never for its own sake and always in the service of the characters. As the film's action coincides roughly with that of the silent cinema, Truffaut uses the devices of that cinema, and adds newsreel footage of Paris in 1900, the First World War, and Nazi book burnings.

Watching *Jules et Jim*, however, we are also watching the end of the New Wave. The first half of the film, set between 1900 and 1914, moves at a cracking pace; the full panoply of cinematic devices is used, and the camera seems to be as liberated and carefree as the characters on screen. After 1918, as the story becomes more sombre, the characters more anguished, and the clouds of Nazism gather over Europe, Truffaut's direction becomes more conventional, more 'classical', and the pace of the film slows considerably. The Bohemian gaiety of the Belle Epoque gives way to sober reality, while the New Wave has done its work, breathing

Henri Serre as Jim and Jeanne Moreau as Catherine in a scene towards the end of *Jules et Jim* when, as this still indicates, the principal characters have ceased to communicate with each other and Catherine is already thinking about killing Jim and herself. Despite the melancholy atmosphere of the denouement, however, the lasting impression audiences take away from *Jules et Jim* is anything but depressing. The light-hearted exuberance of the first half of this 'hymn to love and life' and Moreau's prodigious performance eclipse the fundamental pessimism. Life is worth living despite everything, provided it is lived to the full.

new life into French cinema in a spirit of renewal and continuity, rather than revolution. Out of the *Cahiers* band, only Godard and Rivette, in their very different ways, were to continue being revolutionaries.

Despite the success of *Jules et Jim*, the next six years were to be bumpy ones for the Carrosse, caught (to mix a metaphor) in the backwash of the New Wave. This did not affect Truffaut alone. Godard continued on his increasingly isolated way; Chabrol, affected by a mania to keep filming at

Jean Desailly and Françoise Dorléac in *Silken Skin* (1964). Truffaut put a lot of himself into the character of Pierre Lachenay (Desailly), as he had with Antoine Doinel and Charlie Kohler, but portrayed him with a lack of indulgence verging on masochism. The resulting film, meticulously directed in 'Old Wave' style and rather sombre, was unpopular at the time of its release, but its reputation has grown over the years. Françoise Dorléac, elder sister of Catherine Deneuve, was tragically killed in a car crash in 1967 at the age of twenty-five, 'an actress', wrote Truffaut, 'who never had the time to become a star', but who nevertheless showed a wide-ranging talent in such films as Philippe de Broca's *That Man From Rio*, Roman Polanski's *Cul-de-Sac*, and alongside her sister in Jacques Demy's *Les Demoiselles de Rochefort*. In 1968 Truffaut planned to put together a film about her, but the project fell through.

all costs, agreed to direct sub-007 spy films; and Rivette's troubles reached their peak in 1966 when the censors banned his film of Diderot's *La Religieuse*, causing both Truffaut and Godard to thunder in print against the Minister of 'Kultur', André Malraux. Truffaut's main project was to film Ray Bradbury's *Fahrenheit 451*, to which he bought the rights in mid-1962. Negotiations with American companies, however, proved to be as long as they were unproductive: *Fahrenheit* was not to be made until 1966.

At the invitation of the producer Pierre Roustang, Truffaut agreed to contribute to *Love at Twenty*, one of the international portmanteau films with sketches by different directors on a common theme which were fashionable at the time. For his contribution, *Antoine et Colette*, Truffaut brought back Antoine Doinel (not yet aged 20) and told the story of his unrequited love for Colette, played by Marie-France Pisier, who persists in treating him just as a friend. The episode was based on Truffaut's own experience, with musical concerts replacing the cinema as the place where Antoine meets his beloved. With the usual team behind the camera, *Antoine et Colette* has been mostly shown as a short in its own right, the second brief episode in 'the adventures of Antoine Doinel'. Just after this, in 1963, Truffaut collaborated with Jean-Louis Richard, Jeanne Moreau's husband from whom she was separated, on the screenplay of *Mata-Hari*. This was directed by Richard, starring Moreau, and produced by Les Films du Carrosse. The collaboration with Richard was to be most fruitful. He became co-scenarist for Truffaut's next three films and later on *Day For Night*, before turning actor to play the repulsive Daxiat in *The Last Metro*.

Still unable to get *Fahrenheit* off the ground, Truffaut and Richard wrote an original screenplay, *La Peau Douce* (*Silken Skin*), which was filmed in late 1963 for release in 1964. Despite the presence of Françoise Dorléac, who Truffaut described as 'an incomparable young woman, whose charm, femininity, intelligence, grace and incredible moral power made unforgettable',[16] this sombre, almost cold tale of middle-class adultery is probably Truffaut's least loved film. In particular, the violent ending when the wronged wife (Nelly Benedetti) shoots her adulterous husband (Jean Desailly) was judged to be too melodramatic, despite its being based on a real event. It is certainly Truffaut's darkest film, and stylistically marks the end of the New Wave. The direction is rigorously classical and there is virtually no humour in the film. The detractors of the New Wave were delighted: the new lions were making films in the same way as the old dogs. A film, however, should not be condemned for what it is not, only judged for what it is. Looked at in this way, *Silken Skin*, though it cannot be ranked among Truffaut's best, is perfectly consistent with his themes and preoccupations. After the 'impossible trio' of *Jules et Jim*, the 'impossible couple' had taken their place in his work.

THE MID-1960S — THE 'HITCHBOOK', HOLLYWOOD AND *FAHRENHEIT 451*

Truffaut's greatest achievement between *Jules et Jim* and *Fahrenheit*, however, was not a film but a book: *The Cinema According to Alfred Hitchcock*, better known simply as 'Hitchcock/Truffaut', or by Truffaut himself as 'the Hitchbook'. Truffaut devoted four years of effort and energy to it. His interviews with Hitchcock, which became more like conversations, were arranged by Helen Scott and published simultaneously by Robert Lafont in Paris and Simon and Schuster in New York. Truffaut's formidable knowledge of Hitchcock's output and his boundless enthusiasm for his films got the best out of the Master, who very quickly overcame his initial reticence and his natural propensity to play the role of 'Hitchcock', as seen on TV. Truffaut put the same amount of effort into the illustrations, scouring the cinématheques of Europe for stills from Hitchcock's early British films. The result is undoubtedly one of the best books ever written about the cinema, if not *the* very best. Hitchcock and Truffaut stick to practical matters, the nuts and bolts of film-making, with 'Hitch' explaining to 'François, my boy' how and why he made particular films and individual scenes the way he did. Hitchcock is clearly delighted at being able to explain his methods to his young admirer at a time when critics were tending to write him off. Truffaut planned to do a similar book with Hawks. This unfortunately came to nothing, but the 'definitive' edition of 'the Hitchbook' appeared in a sumptuous edition just before his death. One of his last public appearances was to present this on Bernard Pivot's immensely popular TV programme, *Apostrophes*.

Truffaut was by now a familiar figure in Los Angeles, vainly pursuing negotiations with the studios over *Fahrenheit* while interviewing Hitchcock and even taking language courses to improve his English. He always stayed at the very chic Beverley Hills Hotel, spending many happy hours reading by the poolside (but never in the pool: he was mortally afraid of water). However, the Hollywood social scene was not for the modest Truffaut. At the few parties he attended he was shy and gauche – a situation he treated with great humour in his letters. He preferred the company of the French colony – Jean and Dido Renoir or Leslie Caron – or to meet the great directors of the old school, George Cukor or King Vidor. Later in the 1970s he would fly to Los Angeles after completion of a film to spend two weeks with Renoir, talking about the film he had just made and his future plans. Renoir, in fact, was his last spiritual father, just as the Carrosse was the realization of a dream Renoir had never been able to attain, an independent production company with total artistic freedom.

While Truffaut was spending so much time in Los Angeles, the serious possibility of his working in America was proposed for the first and last time. David Newman and Robert Benton had written the script for *Bonnie and Clyde* with Truffaut in mind. He read the script, had it translated into French, and made copious notes. A few typically Truffaldian ellipses survived in the film as eventually directed by Arthur Penn. Bonnie reads out her poem in the back of her car and, with her voice continuing on the soundtrack, the film dissolves to Officer Hamer reading the poem in a newspaper and then to Warren Beatty doing likewise in a field. We may speculate on what *Bonnie and Clyde* directed by Truffaut would have been like, but while matters were still under discussion the production of *Fahrenheit* was finally ready to go. Truffaut did, however, introduce Newman to Warren Beatty, and the rest is history.

Truffaut did receive other offers to work in America, but he had decided it was not for him. In the mid-1970s Warner Brothers put forward the absurd notion of a remake of *Casablanca*. This sacrilegious idea was firmly rejected by Truffaut and presumably by many other directors as well. Later Stanley Jaffe, producer of *Kramer vs Kramer*, again written by Newman and Benton, was eager to have Truffaut direct it. As a favour to Jaffe, Newman and Steven Spielberg went through the motions of offering it to him, fully aware that he would decline. Truffaut was, of course, well aware of the many European directors who had found success in Hollywood, but these were people who for political or other reasons had been unable to work in their native countries. Directors from Lang, Lubitsch, Wilder and company in the 1930s through to Truffaut's friend Milos Forman after 1968 had been forced to succeed in America: for them it was 'Hollywood or bust'. For Truffaut this was clearly not the case and along with his insistence on total creative freedom, his quasi-artisanal working methods and his temperamental inability to make big spectacular movies excluded the possibility of his ever directing in America despite the esteem in which he was held there.

Fahrenheit 451 finally started filming in January 1966 at Pinewood Studios, London, produced by Lewis M. Allen with a distribution deal with Universal. The basic script was again by Truffaut and Jean-Louis Richard, with additional English dialogue by the unlikely combination of David Rudkin and Helen Scott. The indispensable Suzanne Schiffman, who had studied in America, and was married to an American and therefore spoke good English, was along as 'personal assistant to François Truffaut', but the rest of the crew were British. The music was by

Hitchcock's favourite composer, Bernard Herrmann. The leading role of Montag, the fireman who becomes curious about the books he is ordered to burn, for which Paul Newman and Jean-Paul Belmondo had at various times been proposed, was given to Oskar Werner, Jules from *Jules et Jim*. It was not an altogether happy experience for Truffaut, whose grasp of English was still not good enough for him to direct easily a film in that language. He spent most of his time when not filming either holed up in the Hilton Hotel or at the National Film Theatre watching movies, but the film turned out to be better than one perhaps has a right to expect.

Truffaut and Werner fell out violently during the filming of *Fahrenheit*, Truffaut's side of the story being that Werner was unhappy that the way he was being filmed was not in keeping with his status as a star. For days on end director and principal actor did not talk to each other even on the set. Also on the negative side, the film does not flow as naturally as Truffaut's French films, and the few special effects (the flying policemen pursuing Montag as he flees the city) are crude and silly. On the other hand Truffaut was enchanted with Julie Christie, both as an actress and as a person, and after some hesitation gave her the dual role of Montag's wife and Clarissa, the girl through whom he discovers the joys of reading. His confidence turned out to be fully justified. He also paid tribute to Cyril Cusack, who plays the chief of the firemen and who manages to bring depth and humanity to what would otherwise be the thankless role of a mere barbarian.

Working in colour for the first time, Truffaut was fortunate in having the brilliant Nicolas Roeg as director of photography. Indeed the whole crew lived up to the high reputation of British technicians. Together Truffaut and Roeg created some memorable images: the fire engines racing along the roads to the accompaniment of the emphatic chords of Herrmann's 'Hitchcockian' score, similar to his music for *Psycho*; the 'book people' in the snow-covered forest at the end, a very tricky and undramatic climax which Truffaut brings off very well. In later years Truffaut grew to dislike

Oskar Werner and Julie Christie in a publicity still for *Fahrenheit 451*. Truffaut was enchanted with Christie, giving her a dual role as Linda Montag and Clarissa, but his clashes with Werner, despite their having worked together successfully on *Jules et Jim*, did not facilitate a project which already had a long and troubled production history before the cameras started turning. It was the last Truffaut film not produced by Les Films du Carrosse and his only experience of directing outside France.

Fahrenheit, saying that after it he seriously considered giving up film-making. But on occasions his self-criticism did become excessive, and a working artist of any integrity is always trying to improve on what he has done previously. For a first film in colour and first made in a studio – a foreign studio in a language he had great difficulty in mastering – *Fahrenheit* is a very honourable effort. It was, however, to be the only film he made outside France.

The release of *Fahrenheit* to reasonable if not spectacular success at the box-office and the publication of *Hitchcock* to great acclaim mark the end of a stage in Truffaut's career. From now on he was to make films at the rate of about one every year (two were released in 1970, while 1974 and 1982 were the only 'blank' years), and continue his activities as writer and occasional producer. The Carrosse was still not financially sound, but this did not stop it producing films by Truffaut's friends and collaborators like Claude de Givray and Claude Berri, thereby launching some significant careers, or helping out the by now 'old guard' of the New Wave. In 1966 Truffaut himself acted as producer on Godard's *Two or Three Things I Know About Her*, although the moment of rupture in their relationship was not far away.

Truffaut's own film for 1967 was *The Bride Wore Black*, predictably a great contrast to *Fahrenheit* but influenced very strongly by Hitchcock. Filmed during the summer and autumn of 1967 on location in Cannes, Grenoble and Paris, it marked Truffaut's return to familiar ground with the usual team, though Bernard Herrmann again provided the music. Truffaut was not happy with this adaptation of a novel by Cornell Woolrych, otherwise known as William Irish. It gave him the opportunity to work again with Jeanne Moreau, but in a totally different register from *Jules et Jim*. Here Moreau sets out methodically and coolly to avenge the death of her husband, accidentally shot dead by a group of drunken revellers. Truffaut came to think that she was miscast, unable to express her natural warmth and vivacity. There is no doubt, however, that the

Book-burning in *Fahrenheit 451*. Truffaut's profound commitment to the value of literature and to freedom of expression is evident throughout his films, and he had already shown the Nazis burning books in *Jules et Jim*. In *Fahrenheit* Montag's discovery of books through clandestine reading echoes Antoine Doinel's cult of Balzac in *Les 400 Coups* and Truffaut's own childhood experience. Literature in Truffaut can be almost literally life-saving, and a society which suppresses or despises literature is by definition barbaric.

Jeanne Moreau, with Truffaut in the background, during the filming of *The Bride Wore Black*. Moreau had been perfect as Catherine in *Jules et Jim*, the role with which she will probably always be principally identified, but after the cool reception given to *The Bride* Truffaut wondered whether she had the right choice to portray Julie Kohler. The real problems with the film, however, lay elsewhere.

men she sets out to kill, including Jean-Claude Brialy and Charles Denner, the future man who loved women, are perfectly cast. *The Bride* was also the occasion of Truffaut parting company with Raoul Coutard, who perhaps became the scapegoat for his continuing problems with colour. The film, according to Truffaut, looked too bright and sunny for a tale of murder and revenge, even one with a playful tone. Almost predictably by now, *The Bride* was a commercial failure in France, but picked up awards in the US.

The Bride saw a last important passenger climb aboard the Carrosse. Gérard Lebovici, who was the same age as Truffaut, had abandoned his intended career as an actor to become an agent. He was known as the best negotiator in the world of the performing arts in Paris. From this time on, it was he who would make contact and strike deals with co-producers and potential distributors. In order to obtain the rights to *The Bride Wore Black* Truffaut had had to borrow money from Jeanne Moreau. Thanks to Lebovici, however, the distribution company Les Artistes Associés was brought into the film along with Dino de Laurentiis, long-time specialist in international co-productions. Lebovici was to meet his end shortly before Truffaut, shot dead in an underground parking lot on the Champs Elysées in an ambush which bore all the trademarks of a gangland killing. Rumours abounded: Lebovici's clients had included Jacques Mesrine, former public enemy number one and would-be author, as well as actors who may or may not have had underworld connections. Be that as it may, Lebovici was henceforward an invaluable member of the team.

MAY 1968 – POLITICS AND *THE WILD CHILD*

With *The Bride* set for release in April, there dawned 1968, which was to be as turbulent for Truffaut as for everyone else in France, but also the year in which he made one of his most relaxed and popular films. Truffaut's explanation of what became the 'events' of May '68 could not have been simpler:

> For ten years France had been governed by an authoritarian and anachronistic old man. This state of affairs, which seemed natural to those who had accepted or suffered the regime of Marshal Pétain, was unacceptable to young French people born after the war. In the France of General de Gaulle one had to reach the age of 21 in order to have the right to vote, while the country became more and more Americanized and a 19-year-old singer, Johnny Hallyday, was a national monument before he did his military service.[17]

As political analysis this is hardly profound, but it does show Truffaut's dislike of Gaullist pomposity and his sense that what was happening was truly significant and not merely play-acting by idle students.

Truffaut's personal involvement was in the trailer to the big film. In early February the government decided to remove Henri Langlois from his post as director of the Cinémathèque Française. Truffaut, who was now a member of the administrative council of the Cinémathèque, led the campaign for his reinstatement and became treasurer and prime mover of the Committee for the Defence of the Cinémathèque Française, of which Renoir became honorary president and Alain Resnais active president. There was, in fact, a case for getting rid of Langlois: his method of collecting films, or rather his lack of method, was chaotic, and many films, stored under unsuitable conditions, had deteriorated so much as to be unshowable. But this was to ignore the affection and respect in which Langlois was held by film-makers all over the world, and nothing could excuse the arbitrary and underhand manner in which the manoeuvre was carried out.

Truffaut thus found himself, for the first and last time in his life, playing the role of political militant. The sacking of Langlois became a symbol of the Gaullist government's authoritarianism, and the demonstrations in his favour drew crowds of thousands, including an unknown redhead from Nanterre named Daniel Cohn-Bendit, who whipped up the crowd with injunctions to free 'comrades' arrested by the riot police. The 'Langlois demonstrations' thus acted as a curtain raiser for the riots of May and June. More significantly for the success of the campaign, it was supported almost unanimously by the cinematic community. The old guard and New Wave were finally united: Truffaut, Godard and Chabrol stood shoulder to shoulder with their enemies of not so long ago. Jean Marais and Françoise Rosay, personifications of classical French film-making, led the demonstrations, and literally hundreds of film-makers, from Chaplin to Kurosawa, Rossellini to Vincente Minelli, and Satyajit Ray to Nicholas Ray, threatened to remove their films to a new private Cinémathèque to be run by Langlois. Finally, partly as a result of the campaign, partly through the behind-the-scenes actions of powerful individuals, the cause was won and Langlois reinstated. André Malraux, Minister of 'Kultur', saved his face.

While all this was going on Truffaut had also been filming the third episode of the adventures of Antoine Doinel. For two months in February and March 1968 he was a militant in the morning, and a film director in the afternoon. But apart from the opening shot of the locked gates of the Cinémathèque and the dedication of the film to Langlois, there is no trace of the events of 1968 in *Stolen Kisses*. Truffaut, along with de Givray and Bernard Revon, decided to continue Antoine's adventures in a light, episodic vein, knitting the episodes together by having him work as a private detective. Truffaut again drew on his personal experience of being thrown out of the army and working in a hotel, but most of the inspiration came from talking to the operatives of the real detective agency on which the Blady agency in the film is based. As the centrepiece in the mosaic, Truffaut was delighted and somewhat surprised when Delphine Seyrig, usually associated with more avant-garde ventures, agreed to play the beautiful Fabienne Tabard, with whom Antoine becomes infatuated. She and Michel Lonsdale, who had also appeared in *The Bride*, make a perfect bourgeois couple of humourless husband and charming, sexy wife. The resultant film confirms what Truffaut later put forward as one of the lessons learnt in the practice of film-making: 'The film we make most casually may perhaps be a world-wide success.'[18] It won a hatful of awards in France, the States and Britain, and delighted audiences wherever it was shown providing some much-needed light relief among the traumas of 1968.

Filming *Stolen Kisses*, however, was only a respite for Truffaut. The 'events' of May coincided with the Cannes Festival, but how on earth could one hold an ultra-chic film festival while the country was in chaos? On 12 May Truffaut installed in the lobby of the Carlton Hotel in Cannes a stand asking for money for the Cinémathèque, now deprived of state subsidy. At a turbulent press conference on 18 May the assembled film-makers decided to close the festival, with Truffaut, Godard, Claude Lelouch and Jean-Gabriel Albicocco leading the insurrection. In the evening they invaded the projection room where Carlos Saura's *Peppermint Frappé* was due to be shown. The demonstrators – Truffaut, Godard, Albicocco, Louis Malle, Claude Berri, Milos Forman and others – held on to the curtains to prevent them from opening; Saura and Geraldine Chaplin, his wife and star of the film, applauded from the sidelines. 'We saw Saura fighting for his film not to be shown! It was a pretty good moment.' Godard, who had by now decided he was a Marxist-Leninist, harangued the crowd with clenched fist raised. Four members of the jury – Malle, Roman Polanski, Monica Vitti and Terence Young – resigned. The next day the 21st Cannes Film Festival was declared closed. Truffaut had disturbed it like never before.

The reason behind Truffaut's militancy, however, was not to make a revolution, but to defend freedom of speech and in particular the freedom of film-makers. It was here that Truffaut's generosity showed itself most clearly. It was at this time, for example, that Truffaut and Berri saved the career of Milos Forman in the murky affair of Carlo Ponti and *The Firemen's Ball*. Ponti had bought the foreign rights to Forman's film, then decided he did not want it and demanded $65,000 reimbursement from the Czech government, which in turn threatened to arrest Forman for 'economic sabotage', a grave crime in a communist country at the time. Truffaut and Berri worked like demons to raise the money, and were eventually successful. Berri, no sooner escaped from the brouhaha at Cannes, was despatched to Czechoslovakia, returning with the world-wide rights of *The Firemen's Ball* and Forman's children, snatched from under the guns of the Russian tanks. The friendship between the three directors was sealed permanently. Even on his deathbed Truffaut was eager to see *Amadeus*, which Forman had just completed, but unfortunately it was not ready in time.

Faithful to his fellow film-makers, Truffaut was also faithful to his cinematic origins. In the wake of 1968 the *Cahiers du Cinéma* abandoned the *politique des auteurs* in favour of supposedly political semiological theory, publishing unreadable and incomprehensible rubbish masquerading as political 'interventions'. Not surprisingly, few people wanted to read it, and the publishing house which now owned the *Cahiers* wanted to close the journal down. Truffaut came to the rescue, financing the *Cahiers* throughout their 'Maoist' period, but without any interference in editorial matters. The representative of 'objectively bourgeois' cinema, himself the object of obscure 'texts' in the *Cahiers*, stepped in where the proponents of dialectical materialism – Parisian style – feared to tread. Eventually in 1978, under the direction of Alain Bergala and Serge Toubiana, the *Cahiers* was to return to the land of the living as a monthly review of contemporary cinema with a wide readership, again supporting the *cinéma d'auteur*.

With the 'events' over, Truffaut returned to filming at the end of 1968, but in contrast to the featherweight *Stolen Kisses* this was to be an expensive Franco-Italian co-production featuring the two biggest box-office stars in France: Catherine Deneuve and Jean-Paul Belmondo in *Mississippi Mermaid*. Based on Cornell Woolrych's *Waltz Into Darkness*, with the action transferred from the American South to the island of

The wedding trap. Marriages in Truffaut films are rarely happy for long, but that between Louis Mahé (Jean-Paul Belmondo) and the mysterious Marion (Catherine Deneuve) in *Mississippi Mermaid* is more agitated than most. Audiences reacted badly to the usually macho Belmondo playing an easily manipulated, rather fragile man and Deneuve as an enigmatic would-be murderess, but *Mississippi Mermaid* is, like *Silken Skin* and *A Gorgeous Kid Like Me*, one of the Truffaut films whose reputation had grown steadily since its initial box-office failure.

Réunion, Nice, Aix-en-Provence, Lyon and Grenoble, *Mermaid* is unique among Truffaut's features in that he wrote the script single-handed, which he later considered to be a mistake. The result was a complete flop. The French public did not want to see Deneuve as a villainess and especially not Belmondo as a weak man, essentially passive and sentimental and easily manipulated by a woman. Belmondo's performance as Louis Mahé is in fact very good, but it went too much against his macho and humorous screen image to be accepted by his usual public. Where the public was expecting an adventure film, Truffaut gave them an intimate story, constantly ambiguous right to the end, of a man and a woman who may or may not be falling in love, eventually bound together by their implication in murder. *Mermaid* is another of those Truffaut films more appreciated in retrospect (though not by the director himself) than when it was first released.

Very disappointed with the reception of *Mississippi Mermaid*, Truffaut plunged immediately into his next film, starting filming in July 1969. It was to be a complete contrast to *Mermaid*: a small-scale, highly personal film, made on a low budget, without star names and in black-and-white. Investors were sceptical, and Truffaut thought of making it for television. The result was a huge box-office success in France and around the world! This may be taken either as showing the unpredictability of public taste or as confirmation of Astruc's view that one can never over-estimate an audience. Either way the success of *The Wild Child* was fully deserved. Jean Collet calls it 'the Truffaut film par excellence', observing that chronologically it comes right in the middle of his career.[19] It was also important for the Carrosse: Claude Miller arrived as director of production and here also as actor; Suzanne Schiffman was now credited as assistant director – the script girl on all Truffaut's remaining films was to be Christine Pellé; Jean-Pierre Kohut-Svelko made his debut as production designer; and above all it was Truffaut's first collaboration with Nestor

Truffaut as Dr Jean Itard with Jean-Pierre Cargol in *The Wild Child*. Despite his vicious portrayal of the French school system in *Les 400 Coups*, Truffaut believed deeply in the value of education and the vocation of the pedagogue, as shown in his own portrayal of Itard and in the role played by Jean-François Stevenin in *Small Change*. In *The Wild Child*, however, the ethical questions involved in the eternal 'nature vs nurture' debate are left open for the audience to decide. The film is dedicated to Jean-Pierre Léaud, Truffaut's own 'wild child'.

Almendros, one of the world's great directors of photography. Truffaut had first met Almendros when he worked on Rohmer's *Claire's Knee*, which Truffaut had helped to produce. Truffaut was to learn much from Almendros, and from now on there is a greater attention to the 'look' of a film – colours, lighting, close-ups of actresses – whether or not Almendros is behind the camera.

For the filming of *The Wild Child* the Carrosse assumed its natural role as a travelling caravan, camping in the little village of La Garde Pont-Mort in the Puy-de-Dôme. Between 1969 and *The Last Metro* in 1980, only the continuing adventures of Antoine Doinel, *Bed and Board* and *Love on the Run*, were to be filmed in Paris. Truffaut had started work on the script of *The Wild Child* in 1965, and produced the final version in collaboration with Jean Gruault. It was based on memoirs written between 1801 and 1806 by Dr Jean Itard, recounting how a wild child had been found by peasants in a forest in the Aveyron and how Itard had undertaken his education. After much thought, Truffaut himself played Itard, which was his first major acting role. This decision, basically taken for financial reasons, was 'more profound than I thought at the time. For the first time, while making a film, I identified with an adult'.[20] Jean-Pierre Cargol, who played Victor the wild child, was a gypsy boy spotted by Suzanne Schiffman in Montpellier. In fact there are only two professional actors – Françoise Seigner and Jean Dasté – in *The Wild Child*, the rest of the cast are composed of members of the Carrosse, including Gruault, Claude and Annie Miller, Jean-François Stévenin, and the sound engineer, René Levert, and assorted Truffaut, Schiffman and Levert children. The film thus represents the Truffaut working method in its purest form.

The success of *The Wild Child*, despite its austerity and non-'commercial' subject matter, seems to have convinced Truffaut more than ever that his way lay in making the films he wanted to make in the manner he wished. It was not an easy road, and he was to experience moments of deep discouragement. Some of his films found favour with the public and some did not, although almost all were popular somewhere in the world. During this second phase of his career, Truffaut was a true 'lone wolf' in French cinema, making films outside and against all the cinematic fashions of the day, and with as always each film as much of a contrast as possible with the one before it.

Truffaut could still, however, make the news in defence of freedom of expression. In 1970 the government tried to ban the sale and possession (although not the production) of the 'Maoist' newspaper *La Cause du Peuple*, edited by Jean-Paul Sartre. Truffaut, again in notable contrast to 'committed' left-wing intellectuals, went out onto the streets with Sartre and Simone de Beauvoir to sell the paper and get arrested. The episode

An uncomfortable Japanese meal for Antoine Doinel in *Bed and Board*. Although Antoine takes the first hesitant steps in initiating the affair with Kyoko, she soon takes charge of their relationship and he discovers that Japanese women are truly, as he tells his wife, 'another continent'. Truffaut takes up the theme of *Silken Skin* in lightweight vein, with allusions to Ernst Lubitsch and Jacques Tati as well as echoes of his own earlier 'failure', including one piece of dialogue transposed verbatim.

ended in farce as the police first arrested Sartre, an onlooker shouted out, 'You're not going to arrest a Nobel Prize winner, are you?', and the *flics* retired in embarassment. Truffaut was no more a Maoist than he was a Gaullist or Pompidolian, but, as with the semiological *Cahiers*, the basic principle of liberty of expression was for him far more important than what was being expressed.

After *The Wild Child*, meanwhile, came a new episode in the ever more lightweight adventures of Antoine Doinel, who had now moved definitively from the worlds of autobiography and social document into those of Ernst Lubitsch and *comédie à la française*. *Bed and Board* recounts the break-up of Antoine's marriage, but in an indirect, humorous manner with lots of minor characters and inconsequential gags, making it a true 'group comedy' and a perfect divertissement between the seriousness of *The Wild Child* and the melancholy of *Les Deux Anglaises*. The scenes in the Doinels' apartment were filmed in Truffaut's own, and the staircase is that in the building housing the offices of Les Films du Carrosse.

THE LONE WOLF OF THE CINEMA

Truffaut had taken a long time in deciding whether to film Henri-Pierre Roché's only other novel besides *Jules et Jim*, because *Les Deux Anglaises et le Continent*, written in epistolatory form, was much more difficult to adapt. He started work on the script in hospital following his nervous breakdown and then completed it with Jean Gruault. The complicated story-line, again autobiographical on Roché's part, concerning the relationship between a young Frenchman, Claude Roc, and two English sisters, Anne and Muriel, resulted in Truffaut's longest film: 2 hours 12 minutes in the full version. Léaud plays Claude, with two then little-known English actresses, Kika Markham and Stacey Tendeter, as the sisters. The Welsh sequences were filmed on the Cotentin peninsula in Normandy, with rather unconvincing results. As well as being Truffaut's most downbeat film, it is also, along with *The Woman Next Door*, his most physical, the sexual encounters of the three principals being filmed with, for Truffaut, a remarkable candour, even if distanced by voice-over commentary. Working again with Nestor Almendros, it was the first film in colour with which Truffaut was satisfied. The problems began when the film was shown to the public. Audience reactions at previews were very negative, and the film was cut to 118 minutes and even to 98 minutes. The full version was only seen in 1984, restored by Martine Barraqué for a Truffaut retrospective at the Prades festival.

Truffaut's position as 'lone wolf' during these years inevitably meant inconsistent box-office performance. So *Les Deux Anglaises* was followed in quick succession by another flop and an international triumph. Truffaut had first read Henry Farrell's novel, *Such a Gorgeous Kid Like Me*, during one of his numerous plane flights between Los Angeles and Paris and had 'seen' Bernadette Lafont, with whom he had not worked since *Les Mistons*, in the title role. Truffaut liked *A Gorgeous Kid Like Me*, and he was right: it is probably his most underrated film. Despite its being co-produced and distributed by Columbia, however, the public had other ideas. But this light black (or dark grey) comedy about a woman who makes her way in the world by exploiting the men who fall for her, despite its apparent heartlessness, is typically Truffaldian in theme and execution

The two English girls (Stacey Tendeter and Kika Markham) and the continent (Jean-Pierre Léaud) in *Les Deux Anglaises*, one of Truffaut's most ambitious projects and, with *Fahrenheit 451*, the most troubled. The long and involved story of the relationship between the three main characters, yet another variant of the eternal triangle, was difficult to render in purely cinematic terms. The film insists on its literary origins, with the opening credits showing piles of Roché's novel and pages annotated with Truffaut's own hand. It is one of the clearest expressions of Truffaut's idea of literature as a way of creating order in a chaotic world and understanding the reality of that world.

and deserves a better reputation. Bernadette Lafont is perfect in the lead and, as with *The Bride Wore Black*, the men surrounding her are perfectly cast.

When *A Gorgeous Kid* was released to general hostility or indifference in September 1972, Truffaut was already filming *Day For Night* in the Victorine studios in Nice. This marvellous tribute to the cinema and the people who make it was to be the big success of Truffaut's 'lone wolf' period. Written with Jean-Louis Richard and Suzanne Schiffman, Truffaut's hymn of praise to the cinema is, like 'the Hitchbook,' remarkable for

Jacqueline Bisset and Jean-Pierre Léaud in *Day For Night*, Truffaut's Oscar-winning evocation of the joys and heartaches of film-making. The film being made here, *Je vous présente Pamela*, seems to be a decidedly 'Old Wave' style French production, filmed entirely in the studio: the kind of film Truffaut was to make with *The Last Metro*, the second of his projected trilogy about the performing arts.

its concentration on the practicalities: actors who forget their lines; the laboratory that destroys completed footage; the cat that steadfastly refuses to drink a jug of milk when ordered to (the original may be seen in *Silken Skin*). Unlike other films about film-making such as Fellini's *8½* – probably the nearest direct comparison – there is little about the director's creative agonies. Ferrand, the director played by Truffaut himself, remembers in his dreams stealing stills from outside cinemas, just as Truffaut and Lachenay had done in their nocturnal expeditions, but in his working life he is besieged by the practical and emotional problems of his cast and crew. And, for all that they can be annoying, demanding and juvenile, Truffaut, it is clear, genuinely likes the actors and technicians who create the wonderful fantasies of the movies, represented here by *Je Vous Présente Pamela*, a costume picture in what looks like decidedly Old Wave style.

The cast surrounding Ferrand-Truffaut is superb, with Carrosse regulars led by Léaud joined by Jacqueline Bisset, Valentina Cortese, Alexandra Stewart, Jean-Pierre Aumont, Jean Champion and a young Nathalie Baye. The great tradition of French cinema (Aumont) meets Hollywood (Bisset), Cinecittà (Cortese), the New Wave (Léaud, Stewart) and its own future (Baye). The two insurance men who turn up on the set are played by Marcel Berbert, executive producer as usual, and Nice's most famous resident, Graham Greene, under the pseudonym of Henri Graham. *Day For Night* is the 'defence and illustration' of Truffaut's conception of film-making and was warmly received wherever it was shown. In Los Angeles it received the highest possible accolade from the film industry in the form of the Oscar for Best Foreign Film, which, albeit that this is an odd award sometimes given to the strangest films, was a source of great pride for Truffaut and confirmed once again his standing in America.

After this success it was time for a pause, especially since Truffaut's next project, *The Story of Adèle H*, based on the journals of Adèle Hugo, daughter of Victor, was causing problems. According to Truffaut, these were mostly caused by Frances Guille, the American editor of the journals. He only decided definitively to make the film in September 1974, because he had at last found the right actress – Isabelle Adjani, who had suddenly become a star in Claude Pinoteau's *La Gifle*. In contrast to his two previous films this was an expensive shoot on the islands of Guernsey, representing Halifax, Nova Scotia, and Gorée, off the coast of Senegal and representing Barbados. The usual Carrosse team was involved, but only a handful of professional actors – the rest of the cast were local inhabitants or members of the crew. The future screenwriter and director Bruce Robinson plays Lieutenant Pinson, for whom Adèle pursues her unrequited love, while Sylvia Marriott, who had played the mother of *Les Deux Anglaises*, is Adèle's landlady in Halifax, Mrs Saunders.

There was, then, as in most of Truffaut's films of the 1970s, an experimental side to *Adèle H*. For the music Truffaut turned to the work of Maurice Jaubert who had written the music for many of the great French classics of the 1930s before being killed in the fighting of 1940. Up to now Truffaut had used either Georges Delerue or Antoine Duhamel for his scores. However, he was to use Jaubert's music, mostly concert music rarely or never played, for *Adèle H*, *Small Change*, *The Man Who Loved Women* and *The Green Room*, before turning back to Delerue for his last four films. Truffaut was very nervous about presenting *Adèle H* to the public, an indication, perhaps, of his continued concern at the absence of consistent popular success. In the event the film achieved respectable box-office receipts in France, though not what might have been expected given Adjani's new status. Success in the US, however, where audiences were seeing Adjani for the first time, provided some comfort.

1975 also saw the publication of *Les Films de ma Vie* (*The Films in My Life*), a collection of Truffaut's criticism, some dating back to the *Cahiers* days, some more recent, and tributes to fellow directors. Wishing to pull a slight veil over the polemics of the past, Truffaut selected mainly positive, laudatory pieces covering the whole range of his enthusiasms from the classics to his *copains* of the New Wave. He even included praise of Godard, even though relations between the two directors had broken down irredeemably, more as a result of Godard's bad treatment of Jean-Pierre Léaud than of his militant posturings. Truffaut had never stopped writing, nor was he ever to do so. As one of the literary executors of André Bazin he helped supervise and wrote prefaces for collections of the writings of the man who had 'saved his life'. And in addition he produced a seemingly endless stream of reviews and articles for magazines and newspapers, tributes to directors and actors, prefaces for books on the cinema and reissues of novels by his favourite authors, and pieces for the programmes of ciné-clubs. This last was part of his duties as President of the International Federation of Ciné-Clubs. Heterogeneous as they are, his writings express a consistent view about the moral mission of the cinema, his undiminished enthusiasm for films and books, and his own pleasure in the act of writing. A second collection, half-planned by Truffaut himself and including some of his more polemical pieces, was published posthumously as *Le Plaisir des Yeux* in 1987.

As if to confirm his solitary position and independence in the mid-1970s, Truffaut's next three films after *Adèle H* were all very personal small-scale works, produced by the Carrosse and Artistes Associés. *Small*

Isabelle Adjani, Truffaut and Nestor Almendros at work on *The Story of Adèle H*. 'The film *Adèle*', wrote Truffaut, 'became more and more cramped, claustrophobic, the story of a face.' Fortunately, the face was that of the nineteen-year-old Adjani, beautifully and warmly photographed by Almendros. This intense 'love story with just one character' was more popular in the English-speaking world, where viewers were seeing Adjani for the first time, than it was in France.

Change was, as usual, a long-standing project: the interlocked stories of a group of boys and girls, centred around their school and their family problems, and pulled together into a coherent screenplay by Truffaut and Suzanne Schiffman. To make the film the Carrosse rolled into the town of Thiers, self-proclaimed 'geographical centre of France', and following its

Truffaut with some of the cast of *Small Change*. He wanted to make a film *with* children rather than *about* children and had a remarkable and rare capacity to see things from a child's point of view. Few directors in the history of the cinema have had the same gift: Jean Vigo with *Zéro de Conduite*, Satyajit Ray with the Apu trilogy, Spielberg with *E.T.*, Ingmar Bergman with *Fanny and Alexander*. But none has retained the same childlike but never childish or commercially exploitative spirit throughout his work.

usual practice recruited its young actors on the spot, awakening both confusion and local pride in the good people of the area. The principal adult role, that of the schoolteacher who delivers the speech in favour of neglected children at the end, was taken by Jean-François Stévenin, assistant director who had by now proven his competence as an actor. The only professional involved, Tania Torrens, plays a woman with whom one of the boys is secretly infatuated: an unreal character, therefore, and quite logically played by a member of the Comédie Française. Again, the contrast with *Adèle H* is total. Instead of the story of one person, we have the stories of dozens, with the sole intention of depicting the experience of childhood from the cradle to the first lovers' kiss. The unity of the film comes from Truffaut's awareness of what good actors children are.

While *Small Change* was being edited Truffaut received an invitation from Steven Spielberg to play the French scientist, Claude Lacombe, in *Close Encounters of the Third Kind*. It was to be his only major acting role outside his own films. Normally he turned down such offers automatically, simply because he was always busy, but for once there was a gap in his schedule. He knew his next film would be *The Man Who Loved Women*, but the script was hardly started. Furthermore, he admired Spielberg's films, and was intending to write a book on acting, although the project was subsequently abandoned. Spielberg, for his part, had written the role of Lacombe with Truffaut in mind, 'never imagining he would say yes', but wanting, as he put it, someone with a childlike spirit, 'who could totally admit the existence of the irrational'. Throughout the long shoot on the enormous sound stage in Mobile, Alabama, Truffaut endeavoured to be 'the perfect actor', following his director's instructions: 'This actor will not have any ideas. I will perform your ideas.'[21] He did not presume to offer Spielberg any advice, but tried to do his job as discreetly and professionally as possible. Knowing full well that most of an actor's time was taken up in waiting about, Truffaut had taken his typewriter with him, working on the script of *The Man Who Loved Women* and conferring by telephone about the project that became *The Green Room*.

Truffaut returned to *Close Encounters* after finishing *The Man Who Loved Women*, filming the sequences in India, which he enjoyed a great deal, and the sandstorm sequence in California, which he did not enjoy at all. Although it was a mostly enjoyable experience, *Close Encounters* confirmed his desire never to work in Hollywood. This kind of large-scale spectacle was the complete opposite of his own working methods. He admired Spielberg enormously for his ability to command this vast cinematic operation, to stay in command and remain cheerful in the midst of a hugely complex shoot with literally hundreds of people waiting on his every word and so much money at stake, but Truffaut's own brand of determination was of a different order. He could only be happy and secure as a director with the familiar faces of the Carrosse in the streets of Thiers or Montpellier, the setting of *The Man Who Loved Women*.

After the collectivity of *Small Change*, *The Man Who Loved Women* returns to one central character, but this time a man surrounded by women. In the person of Bertrand Morane, played by Charles Denner, Truffaut provides us with a self-portrait as revealing as the younger Doinel. Like *The Bride Wore Black* and *A Gorgeous Kid Like Me*, the film follows a central character who encounters a series of others, all finely drawn, but possibly better than in the earlier films because they are women. In giving the central role to Denner, Truffaut was taking the kind

Charles Denner as Bertrand Morane in front of his typewriter in *The M Who Loved Women*. The film was conceived for Denner, an actor wh natural air of gravity and earnestness avoids all the clichés about the Don Ju Indeed his best-known previous role as a 'man who loved women' had bee. the murdering Bluebeard in Claude Chabrol's *Landru*! In Truffaut's film embodies Truffaut's love of women and words. Like several others, the 𝑖 shows the writing of a book: Bertrand's autobiographical narrative will be ultimate justification of his life and loves.

of risk in casting against type that he always liked, but which had gone so wrong commercially-speaking with Belmondo in *Mississippi Mermaid*. Truffaut liked Denner, who had appeared in *The Bride* and *A Gorgeous Kid* for 'his physical appearance, his feverish eyes, his worried look, but also for his voice, which is fantastic, magnificent, and which I knew would be good to listen to'.[22] This time the gamble paid off. The film also gave him the chance to work with several actresses: Nelly Borgeaud, who he had had made up to look plain in *Mississippi Mermaid* and to whom he had promised a 'sexy role'; Nathalie Baye, the discovery of *Day For Night*; Leslie Caron, the friend from Hollywood; Geneviève Fontanel; and Brigitte Fossey as the editor who believes in Bertrand's book.

The Man Who Loved Women opened in Paris in April 1977, by which time Truffaut was engaged again on *Close Encounters*. He then took a longer break than usual in Los Angeles before starting filming *The Green Room* in Honfleur and Caen in October and November. This was to be possibly Truffaut's most personal film and certainly one of his very best, but also his worst ever commercial failure, as the morbid subject matter was decidedly not to public taste. The script, based on themes from three stories by Henry James but principally 'The Altar of the Dead', was by Truffaut and Jean Gruault; Truffaut himself chose to play the main role of Julien Davenne, a man for whom fidelity to the dead is all important; Nathalie Baye stepped up into the principal female role; and Truffaut's own fidelity was shown by the addition to the Carrosse team of André Bazin's son Florent as assistant to Nestor Almendros on the photography. Almendros's images are magnificent, contributing greatly to a film which, while demonstrating a 'Gothic' touch unique in Truffaut's work, is also exemplary in the clarity and sobriety of its direction. The critics were, for once, unanimous in their praise, even if the public was not greatly interested. The mistake was in releasing it as a big commercial movie: as an art-house film it would have found its proper level.

The Green Room, despite its commercial failure, was a cheap film to make, so it was far from disastrous for the Carrosse. In retrospect, it seems as if in *Small Change*, *The Man Who Loved Women* and *The Green Room* Truffaut is presenting us with a sort of credo – Truffaut on children, women, books and death – before moving on to broader, more commercial territory. After *Day For Night*, a manifesto for the cinema, he shows how the cinema can express the personality of an *auteur* before moving fully into the popular domain. We should not push this too far – all Truffaut's work shows a profound unity of purpose – but there is a sense in *The Man Who Loved Women* and *The Green Room* of a middle-aged former radical coming to terms with his own deepest nature. They are beyond doubt the most auteurist films by the inventor of the *politique des auteurs*.

There remained, however, the question of Antoine Doinel, last seen in 1970 and now revived for a last time in *Love on the Run*. After the sombreness of *The Green Room* Antoine's final adventures were to be his most inconsequential. Colette, his first love, reappears, still played by Marie-France Pisier who also had a large hand in the screenplay, and excerpts from his previous films are incorporated rather unhappily into the main story. *Love on the Run* is an experiment which does not work. The problem is Antoine. The character had failed to develop and had long since ceased being the *alter ego* of either Truffaut or Jean-Pierre Léaud, who had developed into a fine actor, though unfortunately still too much identified in the public mind with Antoine Doinel. The film was a mistake, but probably a necessary one. It marks the end of a period in Truffaut's career, a long phase in which he was on the margins of French cinema. For all his 'name' and international reputation, he had been a 'lone wolf' for too long.

THE LAST FILMS AND PUBLIC ACCLAIM

With *The Last Metro* Truffaut rediscovered the public success of his beginnings in the cinema, a success continued with *The Woman Next Door* and *Vivement Dimanche*. The Carrosse finally became the *Carrosse d'Or*. *The Last Metro* was an expensive film, costing about twice Truffaut's usual budget, and took 14 weeks to film, one of the longest shoots in his career. The Carrosse only provided one-third of the finance, and the last minute withdrawal of the German co-producers meant that Gérard Lebovici had to use all his negotiating talent to find new partners: Gaumont, SFP and principally the TV network TF1 which eventually provided 22 per cent of the cash. Nor was it easy to make. Jean-Claude Grumberg was called up at the last moment to write dialogue for Steiner, the Jewish theatre director hiding out in his theatre, and the indispensable Suzanne Schiffman fell ill and missed an entire month of the filming. This time Truffaut took his holiday in California before supervising the editing.

The Last Metro was the result of several long-held desires. Truffaut had always wanted to make a film set in Paris during the Occupation, depicting the lives of ordinary people and using some of his own memories, such as the illegal growing of tobacco on every available piece of soil and the omnipresence of the black market. He had also long planned a film about the theatre as the second part of a projected trilogy on the performing arts: *Day For Night* about the cinema, *The Last Metro*, seven years later, about the theatre, to be followed eventually by a film

Gérard Depardieu and Catherine Deneuve in *The Last Metro*. Both stars won Césars for their excellent central performances in a film which exemplifies several of Truffaut's main preoccupations: the eternal triangle, the strength of women, freedom of expression, art and life. Depardieu, physically and in acting style completely unlike Truffaut's usual heroes, brought a new dimension to Truffaut's portrayal of men, revealing the vulnerability and 'feminine' delicacy behind a bluff macho exterior.

about the music hall. Finally, he wanted to provide Catherine Deneuve with a role truly worthy of her, as an active, independent, intelligent woman assuming responsibility for her husband's theatre in a situation of extreme jeopardy. To partner Deneuve he worked for the first time with Gérard Depardieu, by then the number one actor in the French cinema.

Truffaut was nervous: Depardieu's physique and sheer physical presence make him the opposite of the usual Truffaldian hero, but he need not have worried. The part of Bernard Granger allows Depardieu to display the softer, feminine side of his persona – which makes him such a great actor – to perfection. As befits a film about the theatre, other excellent professionals such as Jean Poiret, Andréa Ferréol and Heinz Bennent appear along with Sabine Haudepin, who had first appeared for Truffaut as Catherine's daughter in *Jules et Jim*, while the odious Daxiat is played by Jean-Louis Richard, Truffaut's long-time screenwriting partner, here appearing in front of the camera for the first time.

The mixture worked perfectly. *The Last Metro* was Truffaut's biggest ever commercial success: the only film by a former New Waver to make the list of post-war box-office champions alongside Hollywood blockbusters, Fernandel comedies, *Emmanuelle* and the like. It also garnered no fewer than ten Césars, the French Oscars, including best film, director, screenplay, actor and actress. A new phase in Truffaut's career had opened with a bang, and all seemed set fair for the future.

Tragically the future was to consist of only two films, in complete contrast to one another but both popular successes: *The Woman Next Door*, a sombre tale of an adulterous love affair ending in tragedy, and *Vivement Dimanche*, a deliberately lightweight entertainment in homage to Hitchcock, Hawks and the golden age of the Hollywood B picture. Both are built to a great extent around Fanny Ardant, whom Truffaut had seen on TV (though she had long experience in the theatre) and contacted immediately. Seeing her with Depardieu on César night, the idea for *The Woman Next Door* was born, and Truffaut, Schiffman and Jean Aurel wrote the script very quickly. The filming in Grenoble took a mere six weeks in April and May 1981 and the film opened in Paris in September to critical and popular acclaim. For *Vivement Dimanche* Truffaut turned again to a favourite American pulp writer, Charles Williams, and again with Schiffman and Aurel fabricated an excellent screenplay. Nestor Almendros seized the opportunity to work in black-and-white. The filming, again very swift, was done around Hyères in November and December 1982, and with its release in August 1983 another success was in the bag.

The Woman Next Door tells a simple, ultimately tragic story; *Vivement Dimanche* is ludicrously complicated and winds its way to a conventional happy ending. But both show a film director at the height of his powers. The screenplays are excellently constructed, direction and editing show the art that conceals art, and the actors are perfectly chosen. Jean-Louis Trintignant, working with Truffaut for the first time in *Vivement Dimanche*, is the perfect Truffaut hero (he told Truffaut that he could have

Michèle Baumgartner, Roger Van Hool and Fanny Ardant (left to right) in the garden-party scene in *The Woman Next Door*. The apparently trivial incident when Mathilde (Ardant) accidentally loses her dress is the turning point of the film. Violence erupts and love and obsession slip into a kind of madness, just as they do in *Jules et Jim*, *The Bride Wore Black* and *The Story of Adèle H.*

played any of his heroes, and he was right), while this film also allowed Fanny Ardant to play in a light register after the traumas of *The Woman Next Door*. The very last image of a Truffaut film shows the bridesmaids at the wedding of the hero and heroine kicking around the lens cap which has fallen from the photographer's camera. Children playing with photographic apparatus – however unintentionally, it was a suitable picture on which to finish.

Truffaut had undergone surgery for a brain tumour in August 1983, while working on the screenplay of *La Petite Voleuse* with Claude de Givray. He recovered enough to celebrate the birth of his daughter Jacqueline in October and to publicize the 'definitive' version of 'the Hitchbook' in April 1984, but it was only a temporary respite. Truffaut died in the American Hospital in Neuilly on 21 October 1984. Two days later he was cremated and his ashes buried in the cemetery of his native Montmartre.

Truffaut's reputation, certainly in France, has grown since his death: in America it did not need to grow. Indeed, in contrast to what was often the case during his lifetime, France underwent a wave of 'Truffautolatry'. Perhaps it took his death for French film buffs finally to appreciate his achievement. In May 1988 the first place François Truffaut, complete with a fairly hideous bronze bust, was named at Saint-Gratien in the Val d'Oise. The critic Jacques Siclier, who knew Truffaut well, has talked of the 'dubious mausoleum' erected by the French to Truffaut.[24] He is right to be irritated. A mausoleum is an extravagance, a monument as much to the vanity of the living as to the memory of the dead. It is the diametric opposite of the secret chapels of *The Green Room* where Truffaut/Davenne guards the memory of 'his' dead.

Truffaut was and still is sorely missed by those who worked with him. After his death Jean-Pierre Léaud went through some well-publicized psychological traumas, much to the delight of certain sectors of the press, while at the Cannes festival of 1985 Jeanne Moreau organized a special tribute, bringing together the actors and actresses of his films. But for ordinary film fans, selfish as we are, the best comment probably came from Steven Spielberg: 'With his death I feel as if I'm missing a friend. But even more I'm missing the part of him I knew best: the film-maker. . . . Imagine: 1985 will not have one new François Truffaut movie in it.'[24]

3

Filming with the Family

It is ironic that at a time when almost every film one sees is declared to be 'a film by so-and-so', 'an Alan Parker film', or whatever, the inventor of the *politique des auteurs* and hence of the subsequent 'auteur theory' should have been so modest with his own credits. In the opening titles of Truffaut films all we find is a simple 'Mise-en-scène: François Truffaut', in some instances hiding under the screenplay credit so as to be barely perceptible. More than any other director Truffaut proclaims the cinema as a collective art, created by the work of a team of professionals under the overall guidance of the director. The director for Truffaut was 'he who has no right to complain'.[1] If a film turns out badly everyone else involved, the actors and technicians, have alibis: the script was not good enough; the director did not make clear what he wanted; our work was destroyed by the editing; the working conditions were impossible; we were not allowed the necessary means or freedom to do our best work. The director, however, has no such excuses. He has the duty to take ultimate responsibility for what happens on the set, in the editing room, and when the film is presented to the public. Truffaut was consistent in his adherence to the morality of the *politique des auteurs*, even if the theory did not interest him.

Such a conception of film-making could only apply to independent productions in which the director was involved in all stages of the process from the first outline scenario to the finished product and the only limits to artistic freedom are those imposed by the budget and the time factor, but even here control of the purse strings has to be in friendly hands, not those of anonymous money men. Truffaut, in other words, could never have worked for the traditional type of Hollywood producer or studio boss. With the sole exception of *Fahrenheit 451*, therefore, his films were the work of the trusted Carrosse team, and the responsibility for bad decisions over script or casting lay with Truffaut alone. For example, he did not see until it was too late that Jean Desailly, excellent actor though he is, was too heavy for *Silken Skin*, making the film not merely sombre but depressing; that the role of Julie in *The Bride Wore Black* was not right for Jeanne Moreau; that the screenplays of *The Bride*, *Mississippi Mermaid* and *Love on the Run* were just not well enough constructed. After the event, if anything, he tended to become too self-critical, especially if the film had not been a popular success. It was only after the box-office failures of *A Gorgeous Kid Like Me* and *The Green Room* that he seems to have accepted, rather reluctantly, that all his good films were not necessarily popular. These two films, along with *Shoot the Pianist* and more debatably *Silken Skin* deserved more spectators than they got, at least in France.

Everyone who worked for the Carrosse refers to it habitually as a 'family'. Having been deprived of a proper family life during his childhood, Truffaut created an ideal family atmosphere in his film company. He thus worked with small crews, unrestricted by the rigidity of union rules (this was one reason why he did not work in Paris for many years) and in as relaxed an ambiance as possible. While filming *Close Encounters* he was full of admiration for the way in which Spielberg handled the enormous number of people involved, but realized he could never do it himself. Truffaut made small films, even when they were big productions like *Fahrenheit 451*, *Mississippi Mermaid* or *The Last Metro*, not for any intellectual or ideological reason, but purely because it suited his temperament, his way of working with people, and the way in which he viewed human beings. It was his way of preserving a cinema 'in the first person'; an *auteur* cinema but not in any introspective or self-regarding sense, open to human experience and giving full recognition to the contributions, collective and individual, of all concerned; not 'a film *by* François Truffaut' but 'a film *made with* François Truffaut', whose experience and imagination are transformed into something interesting for the audience.

MENTORS AND INFLUENCES

For Truffaut this 'extended family' included the spiritual fathers, the tutelary gods of the cinematic hearth. When faced with a problem of how to film a difficult scene he would ask himself: 'How would Renoir have filmed this?' or 'How would Hitchcock have done it?'. It was not a question of 'influence' so much as 'affinity'. Indeed, according to Truffaut there were some directors who, however great they were, one should take care not to be influenced by, simply because they were so original – Eisenstein obviously, but also Orson Welles, whom Truffaut admired almost unconditionally and who provided an inspirational example for an independent film-maker, but whose style was so uniquely his own that he could not be an influence. Truffaut the critic, we have seen, wanted to learn lessons from the directors he admired, Renoir and Hitchcock most of all. He remained an ardent film-goer and was still looking, perhaps too much, for new lessons and possibly for approval. Is it mere coincidence that the final 'serene' period of Truffaut's career, that of his last three films, came after the deaths of Renoir and Hitchcock? Was he finally liberated from the searching gaze of the spiritual father? The question may be unfair, but it is worth asking.

During Renoir's lifetime, including the 1970s when he would fly to Los Angeles to see him after the completion of every film, Truffaut referred to him as 'the greatest living film director', as if this were a simple statement of fact, an axiom beyond question. Truffaut's profound respect for the artist and the man and the temperamental affinity between the two directors makes Renoir an invisible presence in all Truffaut's films: 'I think that a director need never feel alone if he knows well the 35 films by the *auteur* of *La Règle du Jeu* and *La Grande Illusion.*' Renoir inspired Truffaut's approach to the job of being a film director, the total commitment to putting the best of one's self into the cinema, and his working methods – teamwork; relaxed atmosphere on the set; the attempt to give the appearance of improvisation to something which has in fact been worked out carefully in every detail. Above all, perhaps, Truffaut learned from Renoir how to give the appearance of realism to strong, even melodramatic, situations by playing them as simply and in as straightforward a manner as possible, thereby avoiding absurdity and sentimentality. This 'lesson' coincided exactly with Truffaut's own artistic temperament and is visible in his treatment of such 'dangerous' subjects as juvenile criminality, adultery, the extremes of amorous passion, and violent death. Arguably this at times went too far: *The Bride Wore Black*, *Mississippi Mermaid* and possibly *Adèle H* could perhaps have done with being a bit more melodramatic, but this is to wish that Truffaut had been other than he was. The 'Renoir touch' plays its part in the success of *Les 400 Coups*, *Jules et Jim*, *Les Deux Anglaises* and *The Woman Next Door* – all potentially melodramatic or grossly sentimental subjects – because it is also 'the Truffaut touch'.

The influence of Hitchcock is more ambiguous. To ask 'How would Hitchcock have filmed this scene?' is fine as long as it is a scene which would never have appeared in a Hitchcock film, otherwise the danger of pastiche lies waiting for the unwary. *The Bride Wore Black*, as reinforced

Truffaut filming *Les Deux Anglaises* during the summer of 1971. He began this adaptation of the other novel by Henri-Pierre Roché, the author of *Jules et Jim*, in a bad state of mind, conscious of his position as outsider in the French cinema, even identifying himself with Orson Welles and thinking constantly about *The Magnificent Ambersons* during the shoot. This became a self-fulfilling prophecy, and the full version of *Les Deux Anglaises* was only reassembled by Martine Barraqué in 1984. Pictorially, however, this third collaboration with Nestor Almendros as director of photography was an undoubted success.

by Bernard Herrmann's emphatic 'Hitchcockian' music, does become pastiche, albeit pale, toned-down pastiche. Truffaut's view of human actions, and in particular of the relations between men and women, is far removed from that of the Master, and all his admiration for Hitchcock cannot change this. Hitchcock is notorious for his delight in manipulating audience reactions through cinematic means. Truffaut tries this on occasion but his heart is never really in it. He certainly directs audience responses in some of his films, but most of the time he leaves us too much freedom and gives us a different kind of pleasure from that provided by Hitchcock or his true disciples. Truffaut looked to Hitchcock for lessons in 'how to express oneself by purely visual means' and undoubtedly picked up many valuable hints, shown in individual sequences and editing. However, there is in his films a constant tension between this and his literary side, his love of language, and the 'keep it simple' approach of his other mentors: Renoir, Rossellini and Hawks. At its best, as in *Jules et Jim* or *The Last Metro*, this is a creative tension, but at other times it weakens the tension inherent in the story. Truffaut's heroes, like Hitchcock's, are men on the run, but in pursuit of their own obsessions, not to escape physical danger. The positive influence of Hitchcock's more 'obsessional' films – *Vertigo*, *Rear Window* or *Marnie* – operates on a deep thematic level, but its expression in cinematic terms is very different from that of Uncle Alfred.

Renoir and Hitchcock were undoubtedly the major influences on Truffaut's approach to film-making, but his knowledge of the cinema and the demands he made upon it were so great that one could almost say he was influenced by every film he liked. Among the many other directors he admired, however, three must be singled out as invisible members of the family: Roberto Rossellini, Howard Hawks and Ernst Lubitsch. Rossellini, like Renoir, was an exemplary figure in his fidelity to principle, that is, his own conception of making films. Truffaut's time as Rossellini's assistant had shown him the problems of an *auteur* working with producers and provided him with another model of independence and intransigence. For all the *Cahiers* band, and in particular Truffaut and Godard, Rossellini's films had been of capital importance in their logic and simplicity. This logic was for Truffaut the sign of Rossellini's courage. For example, Rossellini was the only director at that time to have shown the suicide of a child, not once but twice, in *Germany Year Zero* and *Europa '51* – something which was unthinkable in Hollywood or the European commercial cinema. In the films in question these suicides are necessary and logical, and therefore they had to be shown, but without over-emphasis or false drama. Truffaut's own screenplays are similarly logical: the basic situations in *Silken Skin*, *Adèle H*, *The Man Who Loved Women*,

The Green Room and *The Woman Next Door* are all taken to their logical, often violent conclusions, without false happy endings, but equally without melodrama or grandiosity. And they are essentially very simple situations. Rossellini's *Voyage in Italy* had been a key film for the future New Wave in showing how an apparently trivial subject could be more profound or moving than a self-consciously 'important' film. Rossellini made little films that meant a lot, and he made them simply and relatively cheaply. Truffaut called his style 'humble': a calm approach, morally based, and without directorial arrogance. Truffaut proved himself capable of doing the same, especially in *The Wild Child*, which in its rigour and simplicity is his most 'Rossellinian' film.

Howard Hawks may seem to occupy the opposite end of the cinematic universe to Rossellini, but in his straightforward approach to film-making and his sheer intelligence the contrast is not as great as it may appear. Truffaut called him 'the most intelligent of American directors'. Hawks made films in popular forms – westerns, comedies, thrillers, adventure stories, even a musical – and for a mass audience, but he assumed that the audience possessed brains, never condescended to the lowest common denominator, was never demagogic, never spelled out a 'message' heavy-handedly, and was not scared to slip private jokes into his comedies, New Wave style. Also, Hawks's direction was always in the service of his actors and characters, never flashy or 'artistic' for its own sake. Like Rossellini, he incarnated a complete lack of directorial arrogance while never ceasing to be an *auteur*. Truffaut tried to be like this as well, but like Hawks himself he found that in the 1960s and 1970s audience reactions were unpredictable. Only in his last three films did he attain the Hawksian ideal.

Thematically Truffaut's most Hawksian film is *Day For Night*: the group of professionals dedicated to carrying through a specific task whatever the odds was a favourite subject of Hawks from *Only Angels Have Wings* in the 1930s to *Rio Bravo* and the later westerns of the late 1950s and 1960s. *Day For Night* reprises the theme in what seems like a minor key, but Truffaut might well have said that film-making is not a matter of life and death, it's more important than that, and he would only have been half joking. More generally the influence of Hawks seems to have grown in Truffaut's final years. The work of the theatrical troupe in *The Last Metro*, staging its play under extremely trying circumstances, is another Hawksian group. *The Woman Next Door*, except for its opening and closing helicopter shots, is filmed entirely 'at eye level', Hawks-style, and Fanny Ardant in *Vivement Dimanche*, while undoubtedly recalling Grace Kelly in *Rear Window*, is also by her sheer panache Truffaut's most Hawksian heroine. Truffaut's affinity with Hawks expressed the practical, down-to-earth side of his nature and approach to the cinema and his lack of sentimentality. Their ways of filming death, for example, are very similar in their straightforwardness and suppression of superfluous emotion – it is shown swiftly, without philosophizing or moralizing. One does not have to be heavy-handed to be serious about serious matters.

In a television interview in 1970 Truffaut stated that the strongest influence on his work at that time was that of Ernst Lubitsch: 'From Hitchcock I learned lessons in effectiveness, with the aim of strengthening the visual impact of a film. With Lubitsch I am attracted now by work on the scenario: how to make it more interesting, how to tell a story in an indirect fashion.'[2] And in fact Truffaut's most 'Lubitschian' films – *Stolen Kisses*, *Bed and Board* and *A Gorgeous Kid Like Me* – all date from this period in his career and show his mastery of 'the Lubitsch touch': directorial witticisms based on focussing the audience's attention on seemingly irrelevant objects within a scene or on indicating what has happened so as to avoid the normal cliché scenes. One sequence in *Stolen Kisses* marries Lubitsch with Hitchcock perfectly. Christine Darbon (Claude Jade) has finally decided to sleep with Antoine Doinel, currently working as a TV repair man. She therefore deliberately sabotages her television set while her parents are away. Antoine arrives to repair it: end of scene. The camera then tracks across the living room showing, instead of the usual trail of discarded clothes, a trail of television parts, mounts the stairs, Hitchcock-style, in complete silence before turning into . . . an empty bedroom! Retracing its last steps, still in one movement, the camera crosses the landing and we at last discover Christine and Antoine in bed together. Similarly economical and Lubitsch-like is the sequence in *Bed and Board* where Christine discovers Antoine's adultery with the Japanese girl, Kyoko. Christine receives some flowers sent by Kyoko to Antoine, which as the petals open out release pieces of paper containing declarations of love. Antoine arrives home to find Christine dressed in a kimono squatting Japanese-style on the floor. The effect is comic, but the camera zooms in slowly towards Christine's heavily made-up face to reveal a single tear rolling down her cheek, and the sequence ends without a word of dialogue having been spoken. Truffaut has moved the story forward quickly, economically and wittily, avoiding the seemingly inevitable and tedious scene of recrimination between wife and husband.

For Truffaut, directors like Renoir, Hitchcock, Hawks and Lubitsch, who had begun their careers in the silent cinema, possessed 'the great secret': how to tell a story by purely visual means. It was a secret that Truffaut, perhaps wrongheadedly, tried to discover, but by his own admission without success. His love of language, specifically the French language, rendered it unnecessary. Hence Truffaut's admiration for

Marcel Pagnol and especially Sacha Guitry, whom no one would claim as great directors in the sense of a Renoir or a Hitchcock. Guitry appealed to Truffaut through his wit, his personal tone and, it must be said, his *esprit français*. 'The genius of Sacha Guitry lies in his dialogue: the spectator has the impression that he is listening to an improvisation.' Or again: 'Guitry's heroines tell lies as naturally as breathing, but they breathe love. The men who court them aspire constantly to find a definitive kind of love, before accepting the provisional.'[3] One is a long way here from *Adèle H*, *The Bride Wore Black* or *The Woman Next Door*, but perhaps not so far from *Jules et Jim* or *A Gorgeous Kid Like Me*. Truffaut learned his lessons from Guitry, but is in the final analysis a greater artist both in his view of women and in his combination of word and image. For Truffaut, the French language in the cinema should combine the witticism and improvisatory feel of Guitry or Pagnol with the simplicity of Jean Cocteau and go hand in hand with the emotional power and visual delight of the images provided by a Renoir or a Lubitsch.

From this it follows that the first and most important step in the making of a film is the screenplay. A great film can only be made from a good script, and all the great directors worked on their own scripts. (In fact, Hitchcock and Hawks both worked on their screenplays without getting a final credit.) The original ideas for Truffaut's films were always his own, but only the script of *Mississippi Mermaid* is all his own work. Having decided on a project he chose one or more collaborators from among the small circle with whom he knew he could work easily and fruitfully: mostly Jean Gruault or Jean-Louis Richard for literary adaptations; experienced screenwriters like Jean-Loup Dabadie or Jean Aurel; or younger members of the Carrosse family like Claude de Givray. During filming any final changes were made the night before a scene was to be shot by Truffaut and Suzanne Schiffman, who from *Day For Night* onwards received the screenwriting credits she had perhaps deserved for some time.

Of Truffauts 21 feature films, ten were completely original scripts, eight were adaptations of novels, two of non-fiction books, and one, *The Green Room*, was 'inspired' by themes in stories by Henry James. Seven of his first twelve films were adapted from novels, but only one of the last nine. In other words, as his films became more 'literary' fewer were actually based on literature. Truffaut never forgot his youthful strictures against the literary adaptations of a 'certain tendency in French cinema'. The most important thing in adapting a novel for the screen was to remain true to the spirit of the author, even at the expense of exact fidelity to the story. Thus he did not hesitate in killing off Anne, one of *Les Deux Anglaises*. Henri-Pierre Roché's novel had been based on fact, and the original

'Anne' had not died; Truffaut was making a work of pure fiction, which in his eyes worked better with her death. On the other hand, he would 'borrow' dialogue from another work by the same author to preserve the tone and enrich his film: already *Les Mistons* contains quotes from three stories by Maurice Pons; there is dialogue from *Les Deux Anglaises* in *Jules et Jim*; and the famous opening scene of *Shoot the Pianist*, which has nothing to do with the rest of the film, is taken from *Nightfall*, another novel by David Goodis. In this sense, *The Green Room* is the apotheosis of Truffaut's method: not an adaptation of a Henry James story but a homage to the author by means of a thoroughly personal 'film by François Truffaut'. Truffaut tried his best to meet and talk with the authors whose work he used, succeeding with Roché, Goodis, Ray Bradbury and Cornell Woolrych, and was anxious that his films should help to make Roché better known in France and Goodis and Woolrych better appreciated in America. As it turned out he was too late in all three cases, but their posthumous reputations do owe something to his efforts, on screen and off.

The road from original idea to putting it on film was in most cases a long one. The scripts were worked and reworked, sometimes by long distance collaboration, and made clearer and more economical. Truffaut attributed some of his failures in the 1960s to the inadequacy of the scripts and from about 1970 onwards took more and more care in their preparation – hence in part the greater involvement of Suzanne Schiffman from the earliest stages. The most difficult part, he felt, was the opening of a film, even though some of his openings, such as *Shoot the Pianist* or the frenetic first few minutes of *Jules et Jim* became almost legendary among film buffs. On *The Woman Next Door*, for instance, Truffaut solved the problem by starting at the end, with the ambulance speeding to collect the bodies of the two lovers, and then introducing the narration by Mme Jouve, who thus becomes an important actor in the story. Truffaut often uses voice-over narration, considered by some critics as 'anti-cinematic', but which in Truffaut films serves both as a narrative device, a way of avoiding laborious exposition, and as an expression of Truffaut's love for language and literature.

If the writing of the screenplay was the work of two or three people working together over a long period of time, the actual filming was the work of a larger but still compact and coherent team of collaborators brought together for a relatively short period of time with a common goal and under the overall supervision of 'he who has no right to complain': the director. As far as possible he always worked with people he knew – old or new members of the Carrosse family – who added to the pleasure of film-making as well as making their contribution to the hoped-for success of the film. For the duration of the shoot the team formed a world apart, with the director, as in *Day For Night*, trying to ensure a relaxed atmosphere despite the inevitable personal and professional difficulties. Writing to the actors of *The Last Metro* just before filming began, Truffaut recognized that everyone was nervous when beginning a new film, but that, being involved in 'one of the rare professions which allows pleasure to occupy the front row', everyone should forget their stage fright and 'imagine that we are all living in *The Last Metro* like fish in water'. The set would be closed to the media so as not to distract from the work at hand, 'and now, let this filming be a *fête* and *que la fête commence*'.[4]

In 21 features films Truffaut only worked with seven directors of photography (including nine films with Nestor Almendros); four music composers, leaving aside Maurice Jaubert (including ten films with Georges Delerue); and six editors, while the production side was supervised by Marcel Berbert and the Carrosse team. But the demarcation lines were not strict and everyone involved was a member of the team on equal terms, with Truffaut as first among equals. Indeed, technicians and production staff were likely to find themselves in front of the cameras: in *The Green Room*, for example, Berbert, as often, had a speaking role, while we also see Thi Loan N'Guyen, make-up girl, Jean-Claude Gasché, electrician, Jean-Pierre Kohut-Svelko, designer, Roland Thenot, co-director of production, Martine Barraqué, editor, Josiane Couëdel, secretary of Les Films du Carrosse, and Gérard Bougeant, effects man. Josiane Couëdel recalls this habit as being Truffaut's way of involving everyone in the film and in her case of pushing her forward, and helping her to overcome her natural timidity, similar to Truffaut's own. Finally, in *Vivement Dimanche*, he gave her a small speaking part.[5] The Carrosse was his 'second family and his little kingdom', made up of people on whom he depended and whom he did everything in his power to help. If his favourite joke was to compare the Carrosse family to the Ewings in *Dallas* (Couëdel was Sue Ellen), his jokes were a way of abolishing hierarchy. In the business of film-making everybody was equal, even if all were not equally affected by failure: the director took the ultimate praise and blame, agonized over failure but also received the Oscars and the Césars, the world-wide celebrity.

COLLABORATORS AND CONFIDANTS –
TRUFFAUT'S ACTORS

Actors who worked with Truffaut all say that he was not an interfering director: the relationship between director and performer was that between two collaborators, and it was the actor who brought the character to life. The choice of the right actor was all important: if someone was right for a role then he or she did not need much direction; if they were wrong then there was little the director could do about it. Truffaut's independence meant that he never had to accept stars imposed by producers: the choice, including the mistakes, was always his. And while writing particular films with specific actors already in mind, he did not let sentiment and friendship interfere with his choice. For example, after *Shoot the Pianist* he wanted to work again with Charles Aznavour, but the right part never materialized, and he was prepared to wait for years before working with Belmondo or Trintignant. For Truffaut a film should work in the service of its actors as well as the characters they portrayed, but for that they had to be completely right for the part.

With regard to actresses there was undoubtedly something of a Pygmalion about Truffaut. Those films revolving around a central female character are, among other things, hymns of praise to the actresses involved: Jeanne Moreau in *Jules et Jim*; Françoise Dorléac in *Silken Skin*; Bernadette Lafont in *A Gorgeous Kid Like Me*; Isabelle Adjani in *Adèle H*; Catherine Deneuve in *The Last Metro*; Fanny Ardant in *Vivement Dimanche*. Truffaut's camera is simply in love with them and seeks to make them immortal. Whose most enduring image of Moreau is not *Jules et Jim*? And as for Deneuve, *The Last Metro* finally allowed her to bury both the glacial blonde and the nymphette sides of her screen persona. Truffaut wanted his actresses to be stars and endeavoured to bring them to public attention without being too obvious about it: hence the successive appearances of Marie Dubois in *Shoot the Pianist* and *Jules et Jim*, Claude Jade in the Doinel films, and the progression of Nathalie Baye from being one of the team in *Day For Night* and *The Man Who Loved Women* to the leading female role in *The Green Room*. And with Fanny Ardant, his last 'discovery' for the cinema, Truffaut succeeded in showing both the dramatic and lighter sides of her talent in *The Woman Next Door* and *Vivement Dimanche*.

The case of Jean-Pierre Léaud is probably unique in the history of the cinema. Other directors have had their favourite actors, to some degree *alter egos*, but in creating Antoine Doinel as an amalgam of himself and

Truffaut (left) directing Jean-Pierre Léaud (right) in *Bed and Board*. Although identified principally with the role of Antoine Doinel, Léaud had by 1970 appeared in more than a dozen films for other directors, most notably five with Jean-Luc Godard. 'Truffaut', he would say, 'is my father and Godard my uncle.' But Godard's supposedly bad treatment of Léaud led directly to the acrimony between himself and Truffaut. Despite appearing in a total of 40 films since his debut in *Les 400 Coups*, Léaud has never entirely succeeded in shaking off the Doinel persona.

Léaud, Truffaut, despite his better instincts, created a persona which Léaud has never successfully managed to transcend. Whenever he was asked to talk or write about Léaud, Truffaut insisted on his quality and versatility as an actor, placing him in the line of 'special actors' in the French cinema, which included figures like Louis Jouvet or Robert Le Vigan whose brand of realism or plausibility was 'anti-documentary', giving the impression of being in but not quite of the real world. He defended Léaud unconditionally against hostile criticism, but apparently in vain. Even today, every appearance by Léaud leads some critics to make the inevitable comparison, complaining either that he is still playing Doinel or that he is not as good as he was for Truffaut.

Those actors who best portrayed typical Truffaut heroes – Léaud, Aznavour, Charles Denner, Jean-Louis Trintignant – are all of a similar type, not so very different from the director himself: physically small, timid but active, constantly on the move, light and quick in their movements, and wearing a permanently worried expression, as if not quite in synch with the world around them. These are the typical Truffaut heroes. The exception to the rule, of course, is Gérard Depardieu. Truffaut did not generally like 'muscular', dominant heroes, and his attempt to use Belmondo against his image in *Mississippi Mermaid* had been unacceptable for a mass audience. For all his physical presence, however, Depardieu's brand of realism is not all that different from Léaud's or Denner's. He brings the same air of distraction to his roles for Truffaut. His characters in *The Last Metro* and *The Woman Next Door* are secretly at odds with the world; they have something to hide – Resistance activities for Bernard Granger, an adulterous love affair for Bernard Coudray – and this double face allows Depardieu to express a restrained violence. Depardieu in a Truffaut film is like a sleeping volcano, erupting when he attacks Daxiat in *The Last Metro* and in the garden party scene in *The Woman Next Door*.

But despite his use of well-known stars and his Pygmalion complex, everybody in a Truffaut film is equally important while they are on screen. Supporting parts were chosen with the same care as the major roles, and 'man in café' or 'passer-by' are as important as Jules, Jim or Catherine for the brief moment or scene in which they appear. While filming the climactic scene of *Close Encounters*, Spielberg had to stop Truffaut's attempts to 'find small moments, unselfconscious gestures that revealed character far away from the linear story' for all the 250 extras playing the scientists.[6] For Truffaut there were no 'extras': he could never himself have directed such a sequence. The influence of Renoir and Lubitsch is evident here. Showing what is happening from the point of view of a minor character, a device used frequently by Lubitsch, can be an original, economical or comic way of advancing the story. The man getting drunk in the café in *Jules et Jim* or the various inhabitants of the courtyard in *Bed and Board* give us a different view of the main protagonists, and while Truffaut did not have a stock company of supporting actors, he chose them with care (when they were not already members of the Carrosse team) and allowed them full expression in a manner more reminiscent of the Hollywood of the studio system and contract players than of French films in general.

Adultery and the 'impossible couple': Gérard Depardieu and Fanny Ardant in
The Woman Next Door. Truffaut wanted to make this film 'like a song by Edith
Piaf': 'cheap songs', says Mathilde (Ardant) during her nervous breakdown,
'tell the truth', and Truffaut made good use of popular songs throughout his
work. The pairing of Depardieu and Ardant, initially a bit of a gamble of
Truffaut's part, helped to impart an undercurrent of violence to this his most
erotic film.

Les Films du Carrosse may have been egalitarian, but it was also a ladder, allowing members of the family to learn about film-making and move from assistant director or director of production to making their own films. Directors to emerge from under its wings include Claude de Givray, assistant on *Les Mistons*; Philippe de Broca, first assistant on *Les 400 Coups*; Claude Miller, who directed his first film in 1976 and finally brought *La Petite Voleuse* to the screen in 1985; and Suzanne Schiffman, who finally made her debut as director after Truffaut's death. In the case of Jean-François Stévenin, Truffaut turned him into an actor in *Small Change* and helped him towards becoming a director. The ideal Truffaut team was like a good football team: established stars contributing their genius to the collective endeavour; a backbone of experienced professionals both behind and in front of the camera; and rising hopefuls discovering the true nature and extent of their talents. The director, to pursue the simile, is thus like a manager, coordinating and giving direction to the talents at his disposition. In this way a film is a collective work of art, but one impregnated by and expressing the personality, viewpoint and obsessions of its director.

This personal imprint is expressed or fortified by the look of a film, the changes made to it during filming, and by its editing. Truffaut's admiration for the films of the 1930s and 1940s made him suspicious of colour. His first three features were in black-and-white, and on *Fahrenheit 451* he was fortunate both in having Nicolas Roeg as director of photography and in the subject matter making realism unnecessary. Pictorially *Fahrenheit* is a film of bright colours and simple contrasts: red and black, fire and snow. He stuck with colour in his next three films for commercial reasons, but was not satisfied with the results, and the return to black-and-white in *The Wild Child* signalled the return of artistic and commercial success. It was only through working with Nestor Almendros that Truffaut finally came to terms with colour: the subdued colours and semi-tones of *Les Deux Anglaises* were a deliberate attempt to get away from the bright primary colours considered normal in period pictures; the careful and varied choice of half-tones in *Adèle H* enhance the romantic, fatalistic atmosphere; and the generally sombre colours in *The Green Room* serve to accentuate the brightness of the candles in the funerary chapel, while the dominant browns, greens and blues give the film its 'Gothic' feel. Truffaut returned to black-and-white for *Vivement Dimanche*, explaining: 'It is obvious to me that the thriller is a genre that should have stayed in black-and-white. . . . There was also on my part a slightly polemical intention, the desire to prevent the disappearance of black-and-white.'[7] Truffaut, Martin Scorsese (*Raging Bull*) and Woody Allen (*Manhattan*), demonstrated the continuing validity of black-and-white in the early 1980s.

Photographing a film and turning a script into a moving picture entailed making choices during the filming, changing particular scenes or pieces of dialogue in a continual creative effort. We see Truffaut/Ferrand doing this in *Day For Night*. In reality he did it with Suzanne Schiffman, reviewing the next day's work every evening and making the necessary changes in accordance with how the film was taking shape. This got rid of any need to improvise on the set. Truffaut only improvised with children: with Léaud in *Les 400 Coups* and later the children in *Small Change*. For some scenes he gave them only a few indications and then, filming immediately, let them adapt to the situation of the scene and use their own words. This was his way of showing his confidence in his young actors, equivalent to the confidence he placed in his adult performers by not over-directing them.

Truffaut is rare (possibly even unique) among film-makers in that it truly can be said that none of his films is too long. Only *The Last Metro* and the full version of *Les Deux Anglaises* are over two hours. It was while working on *Shoot the Pianist* (85 minutes) that Truffaut learned the importance of editing, and of all the teams within a team the editor and her or his assistant was the most important. Between the *Pianist* and *Vivement Dimanche* only nine people in all, six of them women, were involved with Truffaut in editing his films, and he used only four chief editors. During the filming of the *Pianist* Cécile Decugis, who had been responsible, among other things, for *Les Mistons* and the 'revolutionary' montage of Godard's *A Bout de Souffle*, was arrested for sheltering members of the Algerian FLN. She was replaced by Claudine Bouché, who remained for *Jules et Jim*, *Silken Skin* and *The Bride Wore Black*, and who was in turn replaced by Agnès Guillemot for the next four films. Yann Dedet, assistant editor since the *Bride*, climbed the ladder to chief editor on *Les Deux Anglaises* and the next four films, assisted by Martine Barraqué, who was chief editor of *The Man Who Loved Women* and all Truffaut's subsequent films.

The montage of a film began while it was being made. Truffaut filmed a lot of footage and the process of turning this into the final product was a matter of leaving things out, constantly tightening and shortening. Martine Barraqué was present during the filming, making suggestions ('We need an outdoor scene here'), and invariably listened to. A week after the end of the shoot Truffaut had a first cut ready, then he took his customary fortnight's vacation and returned to view the film with a certain distance, placing himself in the position of a critic or a hostile spectator. Thus began the final cut. Truffaut treated his footage without respect, changing the order of scenes, rewriting and dubbing those with which he was unsatisfied, and all the time looking for new ellipses and original ways to shorten the film. The opening shot of *The Woman Next Door* was filmed two months after the rest of the film, to give the whole thing a better shape and construction. In his later films he used more and more post-synchronization, the principal aim being to improve the dialogue and allow the actors to be shown in the best possible light.

Shoot the Pianist and *Jules et Jim* are veritable anthologies of editing devices: ellipses, wipes, irises, freeze frames. All the devices of the silent cinema are used in the service of the New Wave. As time went by Truffaut's editing became simpler and more classical, but he retained a particular fondness for the iris, which narrows the vision of the spectator to a single point, concentrating the viewpoint on the person involved, and for his favourite trick of ending scenes with a short, barely noticeable freeze frame. In *The Woman Next Door*, for example, which is a moderately paced, classically constructed film, he uses these little freeze frames a lot and includes one iris in one the face of Fanny Ardant. The effect is to add a little spice to a conventional linear narrative, but always with a view to showing the actors to best advantage. Truffaut's editing consists of what are considered unusual devices nowadays, but always in the interests of clarity, story and character and never out of directorial egotism. His independence allowed him time to work on the editing, to show the film to friends and collaborators such as Jean Aurel and to take note of their opinions, because Truffaut never worked to a strict release date. The reconstituted full version of *Les Deux Anglaises*, undertaken with Martine Barraqué, was a sort of testament to this work – proof that one can always do better in editing a film and that film-making is a continuous learning process.

In a Truffaut film the three ingredients of screenplay, filming and editing are both complementary and contradictory: each worked against the others to produce a final product meant to be consistently interesting and stimulating. If the greatest sin was to bore the audience, the second greatest was to flatter them, making things too easy and therefore demagogic. Truffaut's high expectations of film-making, his desire to communicate its pleasures and problems while at the same time keeping an audience entertained and interested made him highly self-critical, at times to excess. The *politique des auteurs* led some of its adherents ultimately to ignore the audience, producing a 'take it or leave it' attitude which for Truffaut was as bad as its opposite – the Hollywood marketing mentality which destroyed originality and personal film-making. For Truffaut, as for Renoir and Hitchcock, an unpopular film was a failure, but that did not mean that a popular film was necessarily good. With a commercial flop like *A Gorgeous Kid Like Me* Truffaut could admit that he liked it anyway and try to analyse the reasons for its failure, but box-office failure worried him and he was always nervous when presenting his work to the public for the first time. If the film was a failure Truffaut was letting down himself, all the team who had worked on it, the potential audience, and even the great directors he admired, the tradition of which he wanted to be a part. For him, it was ultimately a question of morality.

4

A Morality of Freedom

Truffaut is often described as a 'moralist of the cinema'. This is true to the extent that he had a high moral view of what the cinema should be. On a personal level, because he had learned so much through the cinema his criticism and his films are charged with a moral viewpoint about the relationship between film and audience. Yet his films are never moralizing, there is no preaching or demagogy, and he never tries to impose a simple moral or message; hence his dislike of demonstrative, high-minded cinema, whether it be the liberalism of David Lean or the 'Maoist' militancy of Godard between 1968 and the mid-1970s. Any cinema which tried to 'educate' the audience into thinking correctly represented the exact opposite of Truffaut's cinema. Respect for the audience meant engaging their interest in a story but not telling them what to think. The ideal purpose of the cinema was neither to confirm an audience's prejudices by following the fashions of the moment nor to insult them or accuse them of bad faith. Cinema should be pleasurable but not necessarily easy; moral without arrogantly occupying a supposed moral high ground. Truffaut's films are addressed to a free audience, ready and willing to change their viewpoint and challenge their own received ideas. They are addressed to people willing to doubt everything except their own capacities. His morality is a morality of freedom.

Truffaut had a positive horror of being fashionable. He was even prepared to abandon projects for fear of being accused of following fashion. For example, he would never have made *Jules et Jim* in the 1970s because he might have been taken for a camp follower of feminism. He would never have been a fellow traveller even of a cause he believed in. If his films are feminist this is because Truffaut's personal outlook includes a sort of feminism arising from his desire to see 'real women' portrayed on screen instead of the usual stereotypes. It is a question of respect for women, not social or political theory, but above all it is a question of being true to oneself and not betraying one's morality and personality for the sake of taking the easy way out, either by presenting sexist stereotypes or by following feminist fashion.

Propaganda of any kind, according to Truffaut, only appeals to those already convinced. It preaches to the converted and thereby cuts itself off from the wider audience. If propaganda films can still be good films, this is *despite* their being propaganda, and due to the talents of their directors and actors. When Jean Renoir saw *Les 400 Coups* he told Truffaut that he had made the best portrait of contemporary France on film. This had not been his intention, but he finally admitted that Renoir had a point. All films are reflections of their times, whether they wish to be or not.

AN 'APOLITICAL' REVOLUTIONARY

Truffaut's attitude is shown clearly in his views on politics and political cinema. In the 1960s and 1970s when asked about his politics Truffaut always declared that he was non-political and had never even voted in elections. Yet he signed the 'Manifesto of the 121' against the war in Algeria, which called on French soldiers to desert, and was a leader in closing the Cannes festival in 1968. In his youth it is clear that, obsessed by cinema and literature, he had had no interest whatsoever in politics, but as an adult, despite his protestations, it is equally clear that he did follow politics closely. Believing as he did in fidelity, friendship and consistency in morality and ideas, and given also his dislike of pomposity and vainglory, it is easy to understand his anti-Gaullism and lack of interest in other French politicians. The only politician he is recorded as having admired is Pierre Mendès-France, the epitome of the centre-left, but more importantly a man who remained faithful to his ideas and consistent in his democratic and humanist outlook. But basically Truffaut was not interested in people who sought political power and domination over others.

Truffaut's problem with politics, especially in the period after 1968, was that he was fundamentally a 'man of the Left' who mistrusted left-wing intellectuals. His interest in motivation, his belief in the dictum of Renoir's *La Règle du Jeu* that 'the tragedy is that everyone has his reasons', and his fear of being fashionable at a time when political cinema was all the rage confirmed his position as a 'lone wolf' in the 1970s, more appreciated abroad than in France. He would never have declared, like the Godard of the 'militant' period, 'I am right and everyone else is utterly wrong'. The only political film of this period that Truffaut admired was

Costa-Gavras's Z, for the simple reason that it was a left-wing film that reached a mass audience. Yet the left-wing intelligentsia looked down on Z, because of its melodramatic, 'bourgeois' and 'Hollywoodian' form: it was not 'revolutionary' in form and therefore could not be truly 'revolutionary' in content. Readers old enough to remember the spontaneous applause which greeted Z in the most unlikely settings will realize that Truffaut was right and the intelligentsia tragically wrong. Truffaut liked and trusted the cinema too much ever to fall into the trap of confusing radicalism of form with radicalism of content.

Truffaut was naturally suspicious of people who were politically committed for the wrong reasons – to appear young, trendy, 'revolutionary' – and who therefore felt it necessary to proclaim themselves loudly as being 'more radical then thou'. It was only in the late 1970s, when the fashionable intelligentsia became sympathetic to right-wing ideas, declaring that all socialist ideas led inevitably to the Gulag archipelago and that their own conversion to 'liberalism' was an event of world-shattering importance, that Truffaut finally came clean about his own left-wing outlook (but not 'belief'). Left-wing politics were no longer fashionable, so it was safe to admit to them, but for the right reasons: 'There is only one good reason to be a man of the Left – because it is more just.' Truffaut now admitted to voting Socialist. When asked whether this was a profession of faith, he replied that it was merely information.[1] Truffaut had a faith in people, but not in politics.

The one political belief that runs through Truffaut's films is an unconditional commitment to freedom of expression, as shown in practice by his opposition to censorship, whether of films or of Maoist newspapers. In *Jules et Jim* he indicates the rise of Nazism by showing Nazis burning books. There is no need to show anything else, because for Truffaut it is evident that people who burn books are capable of the most monstrous crimes against humanity. *Fahrenheit 451* was therefore a perfectly natural subject for him, and it is this commitment that makes the film a success despite all the problems involved in its production. Truffaut's commitment is consistent and total: he shows *Mein Kampf* being burnt alongside more worthy titles, including the *Cahiers du Cinéma*. Above all, *The Last Metro* is, in the words of Hervé Dalmais, nothing less than 'a testament-manifesto in favour of the total freedom of the artist.'[2] *The Last Metro* does have a 'message': 'the show must go on', but more than that, the show *should* go on. Expression, through cinema, theatre or books, must and will triumph over all attempts to suppress it by politicians of any colour. The phrase 'everything is political' – the battle cry of the obsessively committed including the 'revolutionary' Left – occurs twice in Truffaut's films. In *Bed and Board* it is stated by a prostitute in what is probably a dig at the Left in general and Godard in particular. More seriously it is the credo of Daxiat, the collaborationist critic in *The Last Metro* and the only truly repulsive character in any Truffaut film. Daxiat commits the one unforgiveable Truffaldian sin: the repression of free expression for political reasons. For Truffaut the idea that everything is political (if it is not merely a banal truism) is implicitly against freedom of expression and therefore freedom in general.

TRUFFAUT, BIBLIOPHILE

But Truffaut's love of books goes far beyond not wanting to see them banned or burned or even a desire to adapt favourite authors for the screen. His films are full of books; they are films about literature rather than literary films. Books in Truffaut's films are reflections of life, but more than that they are the means by which memory becomes creation. Books, like films, may therefore be more important than real life: this is a question constantly posed by Truffaut, but never answered. There is a dual fascination in Truffaut with the process of literary creation and with books as physical objects. *Jules et Jim*, the Antoine Doinel series, *The Wild Child*, *Les Deux Anglaises*, *A Gorgeous Kid Like Me*, *The Story of Adèle H*, *The Man Who Loved Women* and *The Woman Next Door* are all films about the writing of a book, and that book is in a sense the justification for the characters' lives and actions. Jules in *Jules et Jim*, Claude in *Les Deux Anglaises* and Doinel all turn their lives and loves into novels, and in Antoine's case *Les Salades de l'Amour* is probably the only justification for his irresponsibility and fecklessness. Literature confers a kind of immortality on Henri-Pierre Roché, his semi-fictionalized characters and on Truffaut's visualization of them. Less solemnly in *A Gorgeous Kid* Camille, incapable of seeing the difference between a novel and a sociological study, is amazed that Stanislas is writing about her: 'Ah ben, *merde alors*, you're making a novel out of my life!'. Stanislas's naivety lands him in prison, but the film does not end on this cruel joke; the camera pans away to reveal his secretary Hélène typing his book.

In *The Wild Child* and *Adèle H* Truffaut dwells lingeringly on Itard and Adèle writing their journals, with close ups of the pen moving across the paper and a voice-over explaining what is being written. The feeling is almost religious. The journals not only record experience for posterity, they confer a kind of moral authority on it. Truffaut's camera is fascinated by the physical act of writing. The writer is not a special or superior kind of human being – writing is an artisanal activity and hard work, like film-making in *Day For Night* – but it is a privilege to be able and allowed to do it, a privilege which no one has the right to take away. Whatever the author's state of mind it is a free and liberating activity. *The Man Who Loved Women* is the culmination of Truffaut's fascination with books. Having shown us books being burnt in *Fahrenheit 451*, Truffaut now shows us a book being made. We see Bertrand working through the night at his typewriter, smoking innumerable cigarettes to keep him going, and then with Geneviève as guide he and the audience are shown the various stages of book production. The process is for Truffaut at once marvellous and eminently practical: a book is manufactured by many people and many machines, just like a film, but still represents one person's point of view and personality. The publication of the book after Bertrand's death represents the culmination of his life and provides an optimistic, quietly triumphant ending for a film whose hero has been trapped by death in the pursuit of his obsession. Artistic creation is as natural as life and death; harder work, but more permanent.

It does not matter how serious or 'important' Bertrand's book is. The pretentious opinions of the publisher's readers may be ignored: Geneviève supports the book's publication because it is sincere, and her viewpoint is vindicated. Similarly it is not important whether Antoine Doinel's novel is really any good (judging by the title it could be pretty silly) if it is entertaining and true to the author's experience. For Truffaut there is no 'minor art'. Just as there are no bad films, only mediocre directors, there is no bad art, only mediocre artists. Hence his equal appreciation of, for example, Ingmar Bergman and Sacha Guitry or the classics of French literature and American pulp writers, and his own desire to make films as lightweight as *Bed and Board* and as earnest as *The Green Room* and to complete his trilogy about the performing arts with a film on the music hall. Hence also his liking for the less self-consciously serious kind of French *chanson*, such as 'Framboise', sung by Boby Lapointe in *Shoot the Pianist*. He used the work of his favourite *chansonnier*, Charles Trenet, the epitome of charm, lightness and insouciance, twice, in *Stolen Kisses* and *Small Change*. Trenet's seemingly casual throwaway artistry could be as truthful about lost love affairs or the experience of childhood as could any more apparently 'solemn' works. All worthwhile art, major or minor, Bergmanian anguish or 'mere' entertainment, is ultimately a manifestation of human liberty. Truffaut believed in the moral authority of art, which was a very unfashionable idea in the 1970s. Once again, *The Last Metro*, set during a period when art was the only authority worth listening to, illustrates his attitude perfectly: Bernard Granger comes from the 'popular' *Grand Guignol* to the Théâtre Montparnasse to appear in what seems to be a sombre piece of Norwegian Ibsenism and than takes on a third role as a Resistant; Marion Steiner is prepared to go to almost any lengths to keep her theatre open. In a sense *The Last Metro* is a more serious variant of Lubitsch's *To Be Or Not To Be*, and in its 'trick' ending the ambiguous relationship between theatre and life is resolved in a victory for the theatre over the most repressive modern form of reality.

WOMEN AND CHILDREN

This reality is imposed by an adult, masculine-dominated world. Truffaut's motto to the contrary could be: 'Women and children first'. Childhood was the one subject about which, contrary to his normal inclinations, Truffaut did become a preacher. It shows him at his most passionate and intransigent. Asked to produce a text for UNESCO's 'Year of the Child' in 1979 Truffaut thundered against the sick humour of the very idea when thousands of children were starving to death in the Third World; when the French media were more concerned about the Emperor Bokassa's diamonds than his massacre of a hundred children; when France held the European record for the number of mistreated children; when a 'Festival of Cinema and Childhood', which Truffaut consistently refused to attend, was held annually in, of all places, Teheran.[3] For Truffaut childhood was a blessed state, but also a risk and danger to be overcome in the process of growing up. His own childhood clearly conditioned his feelings about mistreated or neglected children, which went beyond mere sympathy and became identification. It is this personal identification, looking at the world from the position of a child, that makes Truffaut, along with Steven Spielberg, the best director of children in the history of the cinema.

Truffaut did not use children in his films, he made films with children, letting them use their own words, but above all being unconditionally on

Jean-Pierre Cargol, the gypsy boy found by Suzanne Schiffman in Montpellier, playing the title role of Victor, *The Wild Child*. Made in the wake of the financial disaster of *Mississippi Mermaid*, this small-scale, highly personal film, superbly photographed in black and white by Nestor Almendros, turned out to be a surprise box-office success. This first collaboration with Almendros, who had already worked with Eric Rohmer, Barbet Schroeder and Roger Corman, helped revitalise Truffaut's appetite for film-making. Working on *The Wild Child* he felt as if he was reliving the experience of *Les 400 Coups*, with the young Cargol taking the place of Jean-Pierre Léaud.

WC-8

their side. He was accused of ignoring the cruelty of children, but for him this was a myth: children become cruel when they imitate the adult world. Left to themselves they are everything but cruel: funny or more often serious, dreamy or practical in the way they tackle the obstacle race of childhood. As always with Truffaut, what is at stake is the moral responsibility of the film-maker, which is greater than ever when children are involved. Truffaut tried to present children without sentimentality or idealizing them: we do not find in his films the pretty smiles or facile tears designed to make audiences go 'Ah!' and feel the warmth of their own tender hearts. The adult world does not feel tender towards children, whatever its pretensions to the contrary. Truffaut, like Rossellini and Spielberg, recognizes and respects the seriousness of children, especially boys between the ages of about six and fourteen. His one directorial command to Jean-Pierre Léaud on *Les 400 Coups* was not to smile unless told to. Truffaut's children are not ingratiating but challenging.

The power of *Les 400 Coups* lies in the fact that the attitude of Doinel/Léaud is never pathetic or looking for sympathy. The look he turns on the adult world and the audience is hard, and the adult world responds in kind, forcing him into the category of 'difficult child' or 'delinquent'. He is viewed as a burden by his parents and by the state and abandoned to the untender mercies of the penal system. Victor in *The Wild Child* has been simply abandoned; the children in *Small Change* are misunderstood because no one listens to them, but their resilience is such that they get by, despite the adult world not because of it, and Truffaut's camera is not so much turned on them as among them, observant and neutral. The world of childhood in Truffaut is to a large extent a world hidden from the gaze of adults. The famous film director remained the little boy sneaking secretly into the cinema, an activity at once liberating and harrowing, on which Truffaut gives practical instructions in both *Les 400 Coups* and *Small Change*.

Yet for all his criticism of the adult world, Truffaut the autodidact believed in education. In playing the role of Itard in *The Wild Child* Truffaut places himself in the position of pedagogue and uses the device of Itard's journal as neutral or scientific observation to avoid the danger of sentimentality. This leaves the audience free to draw their own conclusions about the ethics of forcing the 'wild child' into the civilized world, with all the pain and anguish that this involves. In the remarkable sequence where Itard punishes Victor unjustly to make him understand that the world is unfair Truffaut affirms that there is a moral sense in humankind which can be and should be awakened and encouraged by education. How much is lost in the educative process is left to the audience to decide: a film is not a sermon. Education should extend human capacities, not limit them, and be based on respect for the child. In *Les 400 Coups* Truffaut shows education as it existed in France in the 1950s in a pitiless light. The other side of the coin, representing what should be, is embodied in the teacher played by Jean-François Stévenin in *Small Change*. When he addresses the class about the respect due to children it is Truffaut, for the first and last time, delivering a message directly to the audience. In the film Truffaut has shown indestructible children creating their own space and living their own lives. Adults owe their children respect and comprehension. Truffaut's view of education is, in the facile vocabulary used by politicians and journalists, 'progressive', but it is also based on the recognition of its limitations: the children that we all once were should be allowed to make their own discoveries of culture, freedom and respect for others.

Jean-Pierre Léaud's small stature and Buster Keaton-like demeanour used to good comic effect in *Stolen Kisses*, as Antoine Doinel searches for the woman of his dreams. In the brothel scene in *Bed and Board* Antoine chooses a very tall prostitute, whom he finds 'particularly beautiful', but who lectures him on left-wing politics!

If there is something undefinably mysterious about children, the same goes for women. Feminists may or may not appreciate Truffaut (a case could probably be made either way), but two things are clear in his films: women are fundamentally different from men and they do not conform to male stereotypes. Jules and Jim go off in search of an ideal of feminine beauty but encounter Catherine, a real women who lives by no rules but her own and leads the males a merry dance. Women are possibly magic, often enigmatic, and always stronger than men, possessing secrets that men cannot understand. The young Truffaut, like Bernard in *The Woman Next Door*, must have thought that 'extraordinary things were happening under women's skirts'. *Les Mistons*, as they spy on Bernadette playing tennis or riding her bike, are in thrall to female sensuality. Later, for the still-adolescent Antoine Doinel in *Stolen Kisses*, women's sexuality is bound up with an idealization of women: the beautiful Fabienne Tabard is 'not a woman but a vision', and in her presence Antoine becomes shy, awkward and ridiculous. A lot of the adolescent remains in Truffaut's adult males. For all his dislike of 'psychology' in films, Truffaut portrays men's developing attitude towards women with honesty and acuteness for the simple reason that he put so much of himself in his male protagonists.

The typical Truffaut hero, like Hitchcock's but for different reasons, is a man on the run. It is hard to imagine Antoine Doinel remaining still for five minutes. Truffaut's heroes want to belong in a society that has no place for them unless they renounce their obsessions and change their characters. Their work, unless it is writing, film-making or the theatre, is not serious: at best all it can do is keep alive the perpetual child inside them. The supposedly serious scientific work of Antoine in *Bed and Board*, Bertrand in *The Man Who Loved Women* and Bernard in *The Woman Next Door* seems to be merely a grown-up way of playing with model boats or planes. Julien Davenne in *The Green Room* works half-heartedly for a run-down provincial journal that is like himself an anachronism in the world after the First World War. What is important in their lives lies outside the world of work and it is here that they spring, usually somewhat chaotically, into action.

Dressed to kill. Julie Kohler (Jeanne Moreau) goes about her murderous business in *The Bride Wore Black*. Julie is the most extreme of Truffaut's obsessional heroes and heroines, taking fidelity to her dead husband to barbarous excess. Her male victims, however, are all in their different ways vain and more or less ridiculous: taken collectively they are the least sympathetic of Truffaut's child-men.

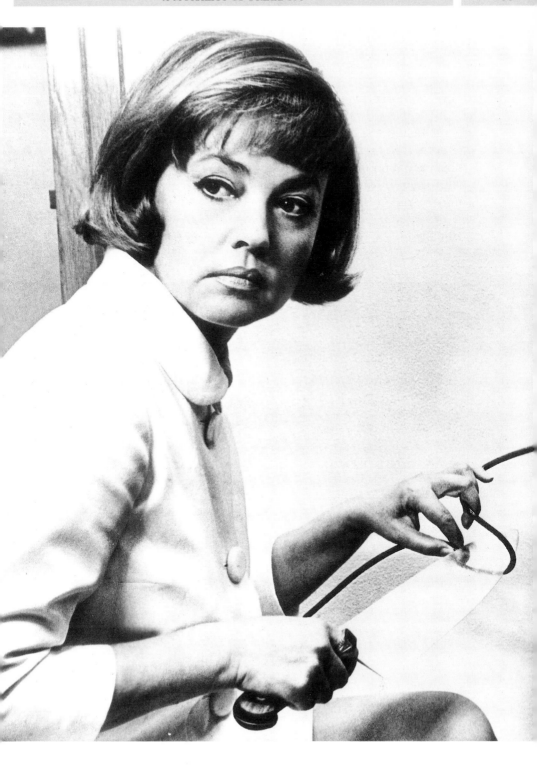

Women are indeed different – calmer, more methodical but at the same time more mysterious. They make the decisions; they take the lead and men follow. 'Women's legs', says Bertrand Morane, 'are the compasses that measure the Earth.' Léna in *Shoot the Pianist* takes Charlie Kohler in hand to get him to return to his career as a concert pianist; Catherine in *Jules et Jim* takes all the important initiatives, including the final one to kill herself and Jim; Antoine Doinel's whole life is spent in pursuit of women who are stronger and more mature than him, and so on. Women possess a logic, which may be wisdom, and which makes them see clearer than men; men are left wondering whether women are magic. Perhaps so, perhaps not, but what is certain is that they have the mysterious power to set the stories moving for Truffaut films and that the actresses who bring them to life have an ungraspable mystery. The movie camera may run after them, like *The Man Who Loved Women*, and turn them into objects of adoration, but it can never penetrate their innermost secrets, never possess them any more than a man can ever possess a woman.

When it comes to presenting women on the screen Truffaut is the least pretentious of film-makers. He never claims a godlike understanding of motivations or 'the female mind'. There is much that remains hidden, which gives his films a ring of truth, of rightness. This fits in perfectly with his fascination with clandestinity: if the cinema for the child Truffaut was a clandestine and guilty pleasure, the same 'Hitchcockian' notion of clandestinity runs through his films, sometimes seriously, sometimes comically. Truffaldian clandestinity starts in childhood. Antoine Doinel's life and feelings take shape unbeknownst to his parents and teachers, from whom he is constantly hiding, with the result that he becomes a criminal and is branded as irredeemably delinquent. Similarly in *Small Change* children pursue their own secret lives, either in humorous vein or potentially tragically as in the case of Julien Leclou who is mistreated by his mother and grandmother without either his school friends or his teachers knowing anything about it.

Truffaut's protagonists lead secret lives either through choice or necessity, through timidity or in pursuit of their obsessions. Adultery in *Silken Skin, Bed and Board, The Man Who Loved Women* and *The Woman Next Door* leads people into secret lives where the serious, the fear of getting caught, goes hand in hand with the absurd, the lengths to which illicit lovers have to go in order to spend time together. Completely 'ordinary' settled people with regulated respectable lives are placed in the position of criminals, leading double lives unknown to their spouses and those closest to them who think they know them. Truffaut's most mysterious women carry their secret lives with them: Julie in *The Bride Wore Black*, Marion in *Mississippi Mermaid* and Adèle Hugo are never what they seem, their reality is hidden from all but themselves. With men, however, the clandestinity is more literal: Charlie Kohler in *Shoot the Pianist* is living under an assumed identity to escape his past; Montag in *Fahrenheit 451* has to lead a double life once he starts taking an interest in the books he is supposed to burn; Julien Davenne's 'real life', centred around his Green Room, is hidden even from his closest friends. These men all choose to be clandestine.

In *The Last Metro* and *Vivement Dimanche*, however, clandestinity is forced upon Lucas Steiner and Julien Vercel, in the first case by repressive politics, in the second by a Hitchcockian combination of circumstances. The man is hidden and passive, so the woman, Marion Steiner or Barbara Becker, takes the active role with competence and

Truffaut directing Catherine Deneuve in *The Last Metro*. The film turned out to be an important one for both director and star, providing Truffaut with his biggest ever popular success and helping establish Deneuve's new 'mature' image. Having named his film company after Jean Renoir's *Le Carrosse d'Or*. Truffaut now tackled the theme of Renoir's masterpiece, the relationship between theatre and real life.

commitment. *The Last Metro* may be deadly serious and *Vivement Dimanche* a featherweight entertainment, but the basic situation is similar and its clarity thoroughly suited to Truffaut's last tributes to women as leaders of the game of life. For Truffaut, being free means being clandestine, keeping a part of one's life hidden from public and private gaze, and the voluntary clandestinity of his characters is never condemned. In *The Last Metro* the point is made political; elsewhere it is more general, part of being a free moral agent.

FIDELITY AND OBSESSION

But there is a price to be paid. In matters of love and feelings we are not free agents: these have a logic of their own which leads to obsession. In the words of the song, 'Love Hurts'. Madame Jouve provides an epitaph for Bertrand and Mathilde in *The Woman Next Door*: 'Neither with you, nor without you': men and women cannot live with each other, nor without each other. Truffaut is the great film-maker of 'the impossible couple' – sometimes 'the impossible trio' – and he follows love affairs with implacable logic, without psychologizing or moralizing, through to their inevitable bad endings. Of all Truffaut's films only the deliberately unrealistic *Vivement Dimanche* has a conventional happy ending, with hero and heroine getting married. But, as Sacha Guitry once said, a comedy that ends in marriage is the beginning of a tragedy. Marriage is no solution, neither is adultery: for Truffaut's men and women both are traps. The marriages in *Silken Skin* and *The Women Next Door* are not excessively unhappy; they are merely shoved into the background by the eruption of real passion into 'normal' lives. There are no guilty parties involved – Truffaut is no dupe of the idea that a husband's adultery is really his wife's fault – circumstances are just like that. There comes a time when even the best of marriages is not enough; human passions cannot be regulated by laws and conventions. Louis Mahé in *Mississippi Mermaid* loves Marion even though she runs out on him and even tries to kill him, but perhaps she loves him too. They are still married at the end of the film, truly bound together until death do them part, but we have no idea what their future may be.

Yet there is also an intense desire to belong to a family: Antoine Doinel, rejected by his own parents, is accepted by and gets on well with the parents of Colette in *Antoine and Colette* and Christine in *Stolen Kisses*. But his own attempts to found a normal family are ruined by his own irresponsibility, or is it simply his humanity? Other characters are forced to seek their own substitutes: Jules, Jim and Catherine are tied together

Fanny Ardant, Jean-Louis Trintignant and Philippe Morier-Genoud in *Vivement Dimanche!*, the lightweight comedy-thriller, replete with Hitchcockian and Hawksian echoes, which offered Ardant a more cheerful role after the solemnity of *The Woman Next Door* and which allowed Truffaut to deal playfully with themes he had treated earnestly elsewhere. Heroine, hero and police are here eavesdropping on a telephone conversation in which the murderer is confessing his crimes and making a very Truffaldian speech about women. 'All that I've done', he says, 'was for women, because I like to look at them, touch them, enjoy them and give them pleasure. Women are magic, M. Dalbache, so I became a magician.'

by bonds of sentiment far stronger than any mere marriage; Julien Davenne is tied to his wife by bonds stronger than death; Adèle Hugo pursues an absolute passion into what the world calls madness. This world labels them as rebels or eccentrics, but they have no desire to be so. In these films Truffaut is radical in a way that goes beyond any mere ideology or politics, sexual or otherwise. It goes to the very root of modern civilization and finds it wanting in the simplest human terms. Ultimately the only families that work in Truffaut's films are the artificial communities involved in making a film or staging a play, where the pursuit of a specific creative goal overshadows all their inevitable problems and squabbles.

Yet if men and women are condemned to live 'neither with you nor without you', what fun can be had on the way! Analysed coldly, Truffaut's plots are for the majority thoroughly pessimistic, yet he seems the very opposite of a pessimistic director or maker of miserable films. *Silken Skin* and *Mississippi Mermaid* were unpopular films and audiences found them depressing, yet they are no more inherently pessimistic than the very popular *Jules et Jim* or *The Woman Next Door*. One can, indeed, easily imagine most of Truffaut's popular films made in such a way as to make them unpopular. Truffaut, an unrepentant fan of Hollywood melodrama, knew that unhappy endings are not necessarily sad endings and that happy endings by their very conventionality can be extremely depressing. His great strength here is his avoidance of sentimentality and audience manipulation. The audience's freedom means that they can choose life. An unhappy ending can have a logic, a rightness, that is the very opposite of depressing, and when Truffaut gets it right the effect is of an apotheosis or exaltation of the people portrayed in the film. So *Jules et Jim*, which after all ends with a double suicide and a funeral, is experienced as a hymn to life, a celebration of love, liberty, the pursuit of happiness, and Jeanne Moreau. Women bring love into the world and Truffaut's cinema revels in it. Because he avoids any Big Statements about The Human Condition, his stories are about nothing beyond the people in them. No philosophy of life is imposed upon his characters, only an implicit humanist morality which accepts and observes them as they are, without indulgence or condemnation. If they die at the end, then so do we all.

For Truffaut a good film had to pursue its own logic. Therefore if the logic of love, the end of illusions, the refusal to compromise and accept provisional solutions lead logically to death, then death will not be denied. The death in a car crash of Alexandre in *Day For Night* is a pure accident, such as could happen to anyone, and that of Léna in *Shoot the Pianist* is an absurd injustice, similar to those in Godard's early films and very 'New Wave' in feeling. But these are exceptions. For the most part, death in

Truffaut films is intimately connected with love. The death of Anne in *Les Deux Anglaises*, though not in Roché's novel, is a logical natural death, like that of Davenne at the end of *The Green Room*. Similarly, the death of Bertrand Morane in *The Man Who Loved Women* is a logical accident, provoked by his obsession with women's legs. When death is not an accident but the logical outcome of an emotional situation it is, of course, the woman who assumes that logic. Catherine in *Jules et Jim* and Mathilde in *The Woman Next Door* calmly and without hysteria put an end to themselves and their lovers. The shooting of Pierre Lachenay by his wife in *Silken Skin* may seem to be different, but since it actually happened in the *fait divers* which inspired the story it could not be illogical or unreasonable.

When asked in 1982 what death represented for him Truffaut replied that it was 'a very logical thing, which shocks me when it strikes children', but that the unpredictability of death makes life more interesting.[4] Truffaut's manner of filming death is as straightforward as that of Hawks: death comes quickly, with no dying speeches; often in middle shot or the distance, without sentimentality. In *The Bride Wore Black* the camera cuts or pans away at the crucial moments, a way of infusing a dose of Hitchcockian black humour into an already outrageous plot-line. Yet Truffaut could go beyond his usual discretion: the ending of *The Woman Next Door*, when Bernard and Mathilde make love passionately before she shoots first him and then herself, links sex and death like nowhere else in Truffaut's films. Truffaut, who did not like sex scenes in films because he thought that the real experience of sex could not be communicated on the screen, here uses it to show the ineradicable nature of the passion between the two lovers and the connection with death as the ultimate expression of 'neither with you nor without you'.

Yet in his own restrained way Truffaut films love and death as a kind of liturgy, dedicated to the religion of love. Men and women approach each other tentatively and tenderly. Truffaut liked filming by candlelight and lamplight, notably in collaboration with Nestor Almendros on *Les Deux Anglaises*, *Adèle H*, *The Green Room* and *The Last Metro*. If anything is truly sacred to Truffaut, who had no conventional religious feelings, it is the coming together of human feelings and fidelity to those emotions. So *The Green Room*, which seems to stand apart among Truffaut's films, is in fact by its very personal nature central to his work. Candlelight here illuminates Davenne's extreme fidelity to 'his' dead, to the friends who are no less important to him because they are dead, in a society which hides death away as the last taboo. It is an attitude which Truffaut, without going as far as Davenne, adopts as his own. The conventional pieties are not enough, even when they are not downright hypocritical, and though love

Truffaut and Nathalie Baye in *The Green Room*, one of Truffaut's most personal and deeply felt films, in which he tackled directly the taboo subject of death and remembrance. Rigorous and intimate in the manner of *The Wild Child*, it also showed an unexpected Gothic side to Truffaut's artistic personality. Truffaut's own central performance is superb, as is Nestor Almendros's photography, but for all its admirable qualities audiences were put off by the sombre subject matter. In reaction, his next film, *Love on the Run*, went to the opposite extreme, being lightweight to the point of triviality.

is not stronger than death in reality (it may be in the cinema), 'our' dead are always with us and form a part of our lives as important as the living. Davenne's devotion to this idea is scandalous to the people and society around him, and the cinematic public was not prepared to follow Truffaut's own milder version of this fidelity.

Davenne is obsessed with his idea, and his obsession takes him beyond the acceptable limits laid down by conventional wisdom. In this he is a typical Truffaldian protagonist. If in most Hollywood films tension and audience interest are gained by such questions as 'Will the hero or heroine win?' or 'Will they get out of this one?', in Truffaut films the question is 'How far will they go?'. The answer, invariably, is 'to the limit'. There will be no last minute conversion or capitulation to 'good sense', to acceptance of the provisional rather than the absolute. All forms of compromise (for example, marriage) are unacceptable. Truffaut's characters live their obsessions to the full and will not be deflected from their purpose except by death. The purpose may be scientific, as in Doctor Itard's desire to educate Victor the wild child, but it is more likely to be inspired by love. In any case the Truffaut protagonist does not know when to 'do the sensible thing' and stop. Truffaut shows us people doing crazy things, but he does it in a logical and supremely understanding way. We may laugh with Truffaut's characters in some of his films, but we never laugh at them, even at their most conventionally absurd.

The text by Balzac cribbed by Antoine Doinel in *Les 400 Coups* is called 'The Search for the Absolute'. Jules and Jim search for the absolute incarnated in the smile on an ancient Greek statue and find it in Catherine, who in turn seeks in vain for an absolute ideal of love. If the world of convention destroys two of them in the end, the adventure has been exhilarating and celebratory. Catherine's going beyond the limits is shown humorously when she jumps into the Seine to show her disapproval of male talk about women and when she disguises herself as a man for a joke, but ultimately she is serious in her extremism. For Adèle Hugo, another seeker of the absolute, her 'love story with only one character', as Truffaut described his film, must be pursued to the end, despite the fact that the object of her affections is obviously uninterested in her. Her *idée fixe* takes her outside her family and to the depths of degradation; she lies and cheats, trying to trap Lieutenant Pinson into marrying her; in desperation she engages a hypnotist to try and change his attitude; and she ends up being branded as mad. Her behaviour is indeed crazy by all conventional standards: she goes beyond the limits in every social and psychological sense, but will not be deflected from her obsession.

Truffaut can show his obsessional protagonists going beyond the limits either comically or with the utmost seriousness, but he never judges them. He is looking for understanding but without idealizing them or shrinking from showing the consequences of their actions. Truffaut's manner of presenting Adèle Hugo, Bertrand Morane or his adulterous couples is indeed quasi-scientific, an effect gained in other films by his use of voice-over narration, typically delivered rapidly and in a flat neutral voice, such as that of Michel Subor in *Jules et Jim* or Truffaut himself in *Les Deux Anglaises*. The introduction of Madame Jouve as objective narrator in *The Woman Next Door* was Truffaut's happiest solution to this question, and her own past adds an extra dimension to the story of Bernard and Mathilde. Truffaut was being entirely true to himself in playing not only Julien Davenne but also the scientists Jean Itard and Claude Lacombe, though Richard Dreyfuss in *Close Encounters* could also be a character from a Truffaut film.

When Truffaldian women go beyond the limits they are less tempted by compromise than men. Julie Kohler in *The Bride Wore Black* pursues her murderous mission of revenge with total implacability, and it is only Truffaut's indirect story-telling and Hitchcockian tics that prevent the film from being very heavy indeed. More lightly and entertainingly Barbara Becker in *Vivement Dimanche* passes herself off as a prostitute and generally behaves in a most unladylike manner in order to save Julien Vercel. Camille Bliss in *A Gorgeous Kid Like Me* lives a whole life beyond the limits. Starting off by (possibly) killing her father, she lies as naturally as she breathes (as Truffaut said of Sacha Guitry's heroines); gives her sexual favours without any sense of guilt; tries to kill two people; cheerfully allows Stanislas to be arrested for murder; and ends up with a successful singing career, despite her complete lack of musical talent. This most Lubitschian of all Truffaut films, too often ignored by his admirers, shows the full extent of his debt to the director who brought Noel Coward's *Design For Living* to the screen and himself went beyond all boundaries of ghastly good taste with *To Be or Not To Be*.

Julien Davenne's obsession with death and remembrance is the most rigorous, concentrated and ultimately tragic in all Truffaut's work, only made acceptable by the exceptional visual beauty of the film, its rigour and sensitivity, and the unaffected and restrained sincerity of Truffaut's performance. He shows how Davenne's passing beyond the limits in this most fundamental of domains leaves him tragically alone. Cécilia Mandel will follow him a great deal of the way for her own strictly personal reasons, but cannot go all the way, which can only be to death. When she lights a last candle for him at the end of the film it is a sign of both the beauty and impossibility of his actions. The audience is left to ponder what is right and human about Davenne.

Man's great obsession, of course, for which he will most usually pass the limits, is woman. The consequences for Truffaut's adulterers are tragic, but this obsession can also be comic, at least when the man involved is Antoine Doinel. His obsession with Fabienne Tabard in *Stolen Kisses* renders him idiotic, but she takes charge of the situation and he fulfils his desires. His obsession with Kyoto in *Bed and Board* leads him beyond the limits (and to some very uncomfortable dinners) and destroys his marriage. But Christine will survive her husband's immaturity and infidelity: the progress of her character becoming a mature and self-possessed woman is one of the nicest things about the Doinel series, even when the hero himself becomes a pain in the neck. She also shows how his extreme actions can be prevented from becoming really tragic, even if they inevitably cause her pain and disillusionment.

Truffaut's most complete portrait in this domain is *The Man Who Loved Women*. Bertrand Morane's obsession is both serious and comic and ultimately tragic, but it is above all sincere. He is fascinated with all women, even if he only goes to bed with attractive ones, and he truly loves them. It is obviously in part a self-portrait of Truffaut, but it is motivated by respect for women and is completely harmless. The only victim of Bertrand's going beyond the limits is himself: even the unstable Delphine, after her spell in prison, comes out stronger and apparently cured. For all his success with women, Bertrand is fundamentally a fascinated and somewhat timid observer, like Truffaut himself in his role as film director. His obsession leads to his death in a manner which is more comic than truly tragic. *The Man Who Loved Women* is a serious film (hence the disaster of Blake Edwards's attempt to turn it into a Hollywood comedy), but one that accept that what is most serious about human beings has its inherently comic side and leaves this dichotomy open and unresolved.

The obsessions of Truffaut's characters are all forms of fidelity to a person, an idea or a quest. Léna in *Shoot the Pianist* dies because of her mission to turn Charlie Kohler back into Edouard Saroyan; Jules, Jim and Catherine remain faithful to their idea of love, friendship and freedom; the fidelity of Julie in *The Bride Wore Black* to her dead husband turns her into a multiple murderess; Adèle Hugo is faithful at all cost to a love that is not returned; Julien Davenne puts fidelity to the dead above the needs of the living; Marion Steiner is not sexually faithful to her husband, but more importantly is faithful to the theatre; Barbara Becker risks her life to save the man she loves even though she is not sure whether he loves her. In his life Truffaut placed the highest value on friendship and, as his quarrel with Godard shows, never forgave breaches of trust. This attitude permeates his films. Once again, it is a question of morality, of moral attitudes sometimes endorsed wholeheartedly by the film, sometimes pushed to extremes and left for audiences to contemplate without prejudice, preaching or conventional thinking.

THE CINEMA OF HUMANISM

Fidelity must mean fidelity to the past in the present. There is a nostalgic vein in Truffaut's films, emphasized by several of them, notably *Jules et Jim* and *Les Deux Anglaises*, being as it were in the past tense, told by a voice-over narrator as things remembered. 'Que reste-t-il de nos amours?' sings Charles Trenet over the opening titles of *Stolen Kisses*, 'Que reste-t-il de tout cela?'. What is left of our past loves is, of course, their memory, the very memory that Julien Davenne refuses to confine to the past. A nostalgic streak is probably inevitable in an artist who makes wide use of his own experience, but Truffaut is remarkably skilful in avoiding the sentimental traps of nostalgia. Hence his use of the distancing device of emotionless voice-over, the avoidance of the picturesque in period pictures, and the use of newsreel footage in *Jules et Jim* and the opening of *The Last Metro*. Truffaut casts a cool but never cynical eye on the past, his own life, and films 'like they don't make any more'. The past is inhabited by people, often wonderful people who live in the present on the screen, and all of them, with the sole exception of the unspeakable Daxiat, worthy of our understanding and respect.

And the past is also made of wonderful films which are still as alive as they ever were. It is said in *Day For Night*, dedicated to Lilian and Dorothy Gish, that with the death of Alexandre a certain kind of cinema also dies, but Truffaut himself revived it in *The Last Metro*, openly parading studio artifice so as to provide a child's-eye view of the Occupation, free from obvious moralizing or sentimentality. The past is to be remembered because it is part of us and made us what we are. It is most emphatically not 'the good old days' – no one who grew up in occupied Paris could believe that – and even the Belle Epoque of *Jules et Jim* is destroyed by the First World War and any attempt to revive it by Nazism. But the best of the past lives in the movies, and it is by absorbing the 'lessons' of a Renoir, Lubitsch or Chaplin that that tradition may be kept alive. This Truffaut succeeded in doing, but as a respector of tradition, not as a conservative, political or otherwise. The iconoclast of the New Wave remained a traditionalist revolutionary, challenging all received ideas and easy assumptions in the name of a morality of freedom.

Because Truffaut was both a traditionalist and in his early films, by reaction against the 'tradition of quality', a revolutionary, it is difficult to pin down his influence on other film-makers. As with the presence of earlier directors in his own work, it is probably better to speak of 'affinities' than of influences. Nevertheless, the New Wave as a whole did have an enormous and direct influence on both sides of the Atlantic, helping to define what we think of as the 'look' of 'sixties' films. The problem is that New Wave trickery, the surface tics of a Truffaut or a Godard, were all too easy to imitate, but Truffaut's morality of cinema could only be assimilated by kindred spirits. Without the New Wave there would have been no *Tom Jones* or *A Hard Day's Night*, no *Prima Della Rivoluzione* or *La Salamandre*, no *Bonnie and Clyde*, *Alice's Restaurant* or *Mean Streets*, but equally we would have been spared so much of what now seems most superficial and dated about the films of the 'sixties', that is those dating from about 1958 to 1975.

In 1963 at the summer school of New York University Department of Film Studies the 20-year-old Martin Scorsese stole (his own word) the first two minutes of *Jules et Jim* for his own very first effort at directing, rejoicing in the title *What's a Nice Girl Like You Doing in a Place Like This?* The rapid cutting, compression of a lot of story into a very short time, and at the same time the care with which each individual shot was mounted in *Jules et Jim*, impressed the young film student permanently. The point is not that Scorsese wished to imitate Truffaut, but that Truffaut had shown what could be done. Later Scorsese said: 'There are certain shots by Truffaut that I'll never get out of my system. There's a shot in *Shoot the Pianist* when the girl presses the doorbell while carrying her violin case. He cuts three times, getting closer every time. This shot turns up in every film I make and I don't know why.'[5] The reason presumably is that Scorsese has, as it were, absorbed Truffaut along with many other things, so that they have become second nature to him. The post-New Wave generation (the one-time Movie Brats in America), especially those like Scorsese who went to Film Schools, have seen so many films, American and European, that they are stuffed with cinephilia. In Scorsese we may find (if we so wish) the influence of Samuel Fuller, John Ford, Truffaut, Godard, Resnais, Michael Powell, Hollywood musicals, etc., etc., but Scorsese's films are uniquely his own. He represents a cine-literate generation who have had even more teachers than the young Truffaut, presented more systematically. The 'lessons' (as Truffaut would have said) of Truffaut and many others have been absorbed: they are part of their culture, their beginnings in film, and their cinematic make-up.

In France Truffaut's importance, only really recognized since his death, has turned out to lie in his continuation of a certain tradition of relatively small-scale humanist film-making, free of any illusions about being a rival to Hollywood and equally free of demagogy and opportunism. It is the tradition represented by a Jean Renoir, a Jacques Becker or a Marcel Pagnol. Not necessarily cheap, it can include Claude Berri's *Jean de Florette* and *Manon des Sources*, intimate epics based on Pagnol and

Truffaut and Steven Spielberg on the set of *Close Encounters of the Third Kind*. In what could well be a staged publicity photo Truffaut seems to be offering directorial advice to Spielberg, something he resolutely denied doing, though Spielberg hints at a different story. Spielberg wrote the role of Lacombe for Truffaut, 'never imagining he would say yes', and he turned out to be what he set out to be, 'the perfect actor', his self-contained style contrasting perfectly with the more extrovert 'American' performance of Richard Dreyfuss. The unconscious but deep affinity between Truffaut and Spielberg, most conspicuous perhaps in *ET*, *Empire of the Sun* and *Hook*, relates to the question first posed in *Les 400 Coups*: 'Where is the father?'

expensive to make, as well as more small-scale efforts. It is this kind of film that represents, inaccurately but honourably, 'French cinema' in the eyes of the world. Truffaut's own international reputation has contributed largely to keeping this tradition alive and popular. In this respect he was truly the heir of Jean Renoir.

Truffaut also represents independence and personal film-making. He was a living example to younger directors, showing that independence was possible and that a personal cinema need not be navel-gazing or obscure, but could reach a wide audience. For this, of course, it is necessary to possess a certain humility, particularly with regard to cinematic tradition, and to be open to the world without following fashion. Not all French directors are capable of this, but enough are to keep the prestige of French cinema alive, despite the 'industry', like its British counterpart, being in a perpetual state of crisis. Truffaut represented industry on a modest, almost artisanal scale. His words tend to be quoted by critics as if they were Holy Writ, part of the 'dubious Mausoleum' attacked by Jacques Siclier, and this is unfortunate as it leads to new forms of dogmatism. However, if young film-makers need models they can do a lot worse than Truffaut.

As always with Truffaut, we are dealing with a moral outlook on the cinema, what it can and should be. The last word is best left to his fellow directors. For Alexandre Astruc he is 'exemplary': 'Truffaut constructed a body of work from which love for the cinema shines out everywhere. In all his films Truffaut speaks in the first person. . . . but he succeeded in speaking only about what interests us.' For Claude Berri he was 'the definitive friend', generous with his advice, who defended and encouraged even Berri's unpopular films. Roman Polanski 'loved his passion for the cinema, and there are very few people who have that kind of passion for the cinema. . . . (He) did not make films for money or glory like most directors.' What impressed Claude Miller was Truffaut's egalitarianism: as soon as his ex-assistant became a director in his own right, 'he spoke to me simply as one film-maker to another.' For Steven Spielberg, 'technically he didn't inspire me the way Fellini or John Ford or David Lean did. Truffaut's influence was emotional. . . . He was the least intimidating, and most personal, of the major film-makers.'[6] Least intimidating, we might add, because most modest. Modesty, independence, egalitarianism, intransigence: the 'lesson' of Truffaut remains a morality of freedom.

Truffaut directing Cyril Cusack and Bee Duffel in *Fahrenheit 451*. Despite his lack of mastery of the English language. Truffaut had nothing but praise for British technicians, notably Nicolas Roeg as director of photography, and for British (in the case of Cusack, Irish) actors, and turned Ray Bradbury's novel into a 'real' Truffaut film, full of personal touches. The first text the fireman, Montag, reads when he discovers books is the opening of *David Copperfield*, where Dickens's hero recounts how he never knew his father.

Filmography

UNE VISITE (France, 1954 [unreleased], 7 mins 40 secs, black-and-white, 16mm, silent)

Director: François Truffaut; *Producer and Assistant Director:* Robert Lachenay; *Screenplay:* François Truffaut; *Editor:* Alain Resnais; *Photography:* Jacques Rivette

Cast: Laura Mori, Jean-José Richer, Francis Cognany, Florence Doniol-Valcroze

A young man is looking for lodgings, reads an advertisement and visits an apartment already occupied by a young woman. The woman's brother-in-law calls to leave his young daughter with her. The brother-in-law and the 'lodger' both make passes at the young woman, without success. The two men depart, leaving the young woman and the child.

> I improvized, which is absolutely crazy for an amateur. . . . Anyway, there was no story, it was incomprehensible and unshowable. (Truffaut, 1961)

LES MISTONS (US/UK: *The Mischief Makers*, France, 1958, 23 mins. Black-and-white, 16mm)

Director: François Truffaut; *Production:* Les Films du Carrosse; *Director of*

Production: Robert Lachenay; *Screenplay:* François Truffaut, from a short story by Maurice Pons; *Editor:* Cécile Decugis; *Photography:* Jean Malige; *Music:* Maurice Le Roux

Principal Cast: Bernadette Lafont (Bernadette), Gérard Blain (Gérard), commentary spoken by Michel François

Direction Prize, Brussels Festival; Young Spectators Prize, Belgium; Gold Medal, Mannheim Festival; Blue Ribbon Award, United States.

In Nîmes at the height of summer a gang of young boys spy on Bernadette and her lover Gérard, following them everywhere. They send a 'suggestive' postcard to Bernadette, while Gérard leaves for a mountaineering holiday. Bernadette and the boys learn of Gérard's death in an accident. The school holidays are over.

> While making *Les Mistons* I realized that there were things I liked and things I disliked and that the choice of subject for a film is more important than one thinks and that one cannot enter into it lightly. I realized, for example, that the story in itself did not interest me and that there was no connection between the lives of the

five children and the two lovers. . . .
When I filmed the almost
documentary scenes with the children
I was happy and all went well.
(Truffaut)

UNE HISTOIRE D'EAU (France, 1958,
18 mins, black-and-white, 16mm)

Direction and Screenplay: François
Truffaut, Jean-Luc Godard; *Producer:*
Pierre Braunberger; *Editor:* Jean-Luc
Godard; *Photography:* Michel Latouche

Cast: Jean-Claude Brialy, Caroline Dim

A female student, stranded by floods in
the Paris region, accepts a lift from a
young man. After making their way to
Paris by car and on foot she decides that
she will probably sleep with him that
night.

> I think you'll agree that it is neither
> Godard's best film nor Truffaut's best
> film. . . . I brought back six hundred
> metres of film . . . Jean-Luc Godard
> wanted to see them and said: 'It would
> be fun to edit them.' He did a
> montage of the film in his own way
> and a commentary. . . . It was logical
> to put both our names on it and to
> give it to the producer as a present.
> He did not make a fortune out of it.
> (Truffaut)

LES 400 COUPS (US/UK: *The 400
Blows*, France, 1959, 93 mins, black-and-
white, Dyaliscope)

Director: François Truffaut; *Production:*
Les Films du Carrosse, SEDIF;
Screenplay: François Truffaut, Marcel
Moussy; *Editor:* Marie-Josèphe Yoyotte;
Photography: Henri Decae; *Design:*
Bernard Evein; *Music:* Jean Constantin

Principal Cast: Jean-Pierre Léaud
(Antoine Doinel), Claire Maurier (his
mother), Albert Rémy (his father),
Patrick Auffay (René), Georges Flamant
(René's father), Guy Decomble
(schoolteacher), Yvonne Claudie (Mme

Bigey), Claude Mansard (examining
magistrate)

Director's Prize, Cannes Film Festival,
1959; Joseph Burstyn Prize (best foreign
film shown in the United States) 1959;
New York Critics Prize, Best Foreign
Film, 1959; Prix Méliès, 1959 (jointly
with *Last Year in Marienbad*); Prix
Fémina (Belgium); other awards at the
festivals of Acapulco and Valladolid.

Dedicated to André Bazin.

Twelve-year-old Antoine Doinel has
problems at school and at home, where
his mother and stepfather quarrel and
treat him with indifference. He cuts
school, steals from his parents, cribs an
essay from Balzac and gets caught out,
and sees his mother kissing a lover in the
street. One day he explains his absence
from school by claiming that his mother
is dead, but she appears at the school
and Antoine and his friend René are
banned for a week. Antoine hides in
René's house. They steal a typewriter to
finance a trip to the seaside, but cannot
sell it, and Antoine is caught in the act of
returning it. His stepfather drags him to
the police station from where he is sent
to an observation camp for juvenile
delinquents. He escapes, runs across
country and keeps going until he reaches
the sea.

> Childhood, its ideals, disappointments,
> desires, resentments and suddenly
> changing moods are observed here not
> from the heights of a kind of middle-
> aged prudence, but with humility; and
> with the mischievous charm of the
> child himself. Thus the picture gives
> the audience something of itself: not in
> the form of nostalgia but as a fresh and
> noble souvenir of childhood. ('R.V.',
> *Monthly Film Bulletin*)

Jean Renoir taught me that the actor
playing a character is more important
than that character or, if you prefer,
the abstract should be sacrificed to the

concrete. It is not surprising therefore if, from the first day of filming *Les 400 Coups*, Antoine Doinel became less myself and more Jean-Pierre. On the screen Antoine Doinel became more robust and of such evident good faith that the public forgave him everything to the point that his parents and the other adult characters became almost odious. (Truffaut)

TIREZ SUR LE PIANISTE (US: *Shoot the Piano Player*; UK: *Shoot the Pianist*, France, 1960, 85 mins, black-and-white, Dyaliscope)

Director: François Truffaut; *Production:* Pierre Braunberger, Les Films de la Pléiade; *Screenplay:* François Truffaut, Marcel Moussy, from the novel *Down There* by David Goodis; *Editor:* Cécile Decugis, Claudine Bouché; *Photography:* Raoul Coutard; *Design:* Jacques Mély; *Music:* Georges Delerue

Principal Cast: Charles Aznavour (Charlie Kohler/Edouard Saroyan), Marie Dubois (Léna), Nicole Berger (Theresa), Michèle Mercier (Clarisse), Albert Rémy (Chico), Claude Mansard (Momo), Daniel Boulanger (Ernest), Richard Kanaian (Fido), Serge Davri (Plyne), Jean-Jacques Aslanian (Richard), Claude Heymann (Lars Schmeel), Catherine Lutz (Mammy)

Prix de la Nouvelle Critique, 1960.

Charlie Kohler, a timid, withdrawn pianist in a low-life bar, is forced to hide his brothers, Chico and Richard, who are fleeing from two gangsters they have double-crossed. The bar waitress, Léna, persuades Charlie to talk about his life and it is revealed that he was once a famous concert pianist named Edouard Saroyan. His marriage had ended when his wife, Theresa, revealed that she had slept with the impresario, Lars Schmeel, in order to further Edouard's career, and then committed suicide. Léna promises to help Charlie make a comeback, but

the aggressive and jealous barkeeper, Plyne, attacks Charlie who accidentally kills him. Whilst Charlie and Léna are trying to hush up the crime, Fido, the youngest brother, is kidnapped by the two gangsters and taken to a mountain chalet, where Chico and Richard are hiding. In the ensuing gun fight Léna is killed. Charlie returns to his bar piano.

Shoot the Piano Player is both nihilistic in attitude and, at the same time, in its wit and good spirits, totally involved in life and fun. Whatever Truffaut touches seems to leap to life – even a gangster thriller is transformed into the human comedy. A *comedy* about melancholia, about the hopelessness of life can only give the lie to the theme; for as long as we can joke, life is not hopeless, we can enjoy it. (Pauline Kael, *Film Culture*)

One should not look for reality in the *Pianist* – neither in this family of Armenians in the snow near Grenoble, nor in this bar at Levallois-Perret (people don't dance in such bars) – but simply the pleasure of mixing things up to see whether they can be mixed or not, and I believe in this idea of mélange which, I think, rules over everything. (Truffaut)

JULES ET JIM (US/UK: *Jules and Jim*, France, 1962, 110 mins, black-and-white, Franscope)

Director: François Truffaut; *Production:* Les Films du Carrosse; SEDIF; *Director of Production:* Marcel Berbert; *Screenplay:* François Truffaut, Jean Gruault, from the novel by Henri-Pierre Roché; *Editor:* Claudine Bouché; *Photography:* Raoul Coutard; *Design:* Fred Capel; *Music:* Georges Delerue; song 'Le Tourbillon' by Bassiak (Serge Rezvani).

Principal Cast: Jeanne Moreau (Catherine), Oskar Werner (Jules), Henri Serre (Jim), Marie Dubois (Thérèse),

Boris Bassiak (Albert), Danielle Bassiak (Albert's companion), Sabine Haudepin (Sabine), Vanna Urbino (Gilberte), Anny Nelson (Lucie), Bernard Largemains (Merlin)

Director's Prize, festivals of Mar del Plata and Acapulco; Prix de l'Académie du Cinéma (Best French Film and Best Actress, Jeanne Moreau); Danish Oscar 'Bodil' for Best European Film of the year, 1963; Italian journalists' award, Nostro Argento, for best film of the year.

In the bohemian milieu of pre-1914 Paris Jim, a Frenchman, and Jules, a German, form an indestructible friendship. Their search for the ideal women ends when Catherine enters their lives. She becomes Jules's girl, but they form an inseparable trio. During the First World War Jules and Catherine, now married, settle in Germany, while the two men fight in the trenches on opposing sides. When Jim visits them after the war, Jules and Catherine seem idyllically happy with their young daughter, Sabine, but Jules reveals that he has lost Catherine: she has left him before and will doubtless do so again. Jules watches and even encourages as Jim and Catherine become lovers, because that way she will not be entirely lost to him. But the volatile, unhappy Catherine is too much for Jim, who goes back to Paris and his faithful Gilberte. When, some years later, Jules and Catherine come to live in France, nothing has changed. Catherine makes her final gesture, driving her car into a river, taking Jim with her.

> What is the film about? It's a celebration of life in a great historical period, a period of ferment and extraordinary achievement in painting and music and literature. Together Jules and Jim have a peaceful friendship. . . . but when Jules and Jim are with Catherine they feel alive. Anything may happen – she's the catalyst, the troublemaker, the source

of despair as well as the source of joy. She is the enchantress who makes art out of life. (Pauline Kael, *Partisan Review*)

Jules et Jim ends after the burning of the books in Germany, the end of an epoch, as Truffaut has said, for intellectual Bohemians like Jules and Jim. The film is, in a way, a tribute to the books that were burned; I can't think of another movie so full of books, and of references to books and of writing and translating books. Books were the blood of these characters: they took their ideas of life from books, and writing books was their idea of living. (*ibid.*)

If this film is successful it should be like the book that inspired it and thus be a hymn to love, perhaps even a hymn to life. (Truffaut)

If the director has a definite moral viewpoint to express, it is so obscure that the visual amorality and immorality of the film are predominant and consequently pose a serious problem for a mass medium of entertainment. (American Legion of Decency)

ANTOINE ET COLETTE (US/UK: *Love at Twenty*, France, 1962, 29 mins, black-and-white, Cinemascope)

Director: François Truffaut; *Production:* Pierre Roustang, Ulysse Productions, taken over by Les Films du Carrosse; *Director of Production:* Philippe Dussart; *Screenplay:* François Truffaut; *Editor:* Claudine Bouché; *Photography:* Raoul Coutard; *Music:* Georges Delerue

Cast: Jean-Pierre Léaud (Antoine Doinel), Marie-France Pisier (Colette), Patrick Auffay (René), Rosy Varte (Colette's mother), François Darbon (Colette's stepfather), Jean-François Adam (Albert), commentary spoken by Henri Serre

Sketch in film *Love at Twenty*: other

episodes directed by Renzo Rossellini, Marcel Ophuls, Andrzej Wajda and Shintaro Ishihara.

Antoine Doinel, now working for a record company, meets Colette at concerts. He is in love with her, but to her he is just a friend. He moves in over the road from her apartment, and her mother and stepfather 'adopt' the parentless Antoine. One night as he visits after dinner Colette's boyfriend Albert arrives to take her out. Antoine is left to ponder sadly on his unrequited love.

> What strikes one most of all . . . is the casual density of Truffaut's observation – the way Colette fumbles with a locket when she knows she is being watched, or Antoine draws hesitantly back on a balcony when he desperately wants to be seen; a density which enables him to create living people rather than characters, who arouse interest not because they make a point but simply because they exist. (Tom Milne, *Monthly Film Bulletin*)

> I made it during a carefree moment: *Jules et Jim* had just been released and had been very well received, which meant that I set to work on *L'Amour à vingt ans* in a very lighthearted fashion. (Truffaut)

LA PEAU DOUCE (US: *The Soft Skin*; UK: *Silken Skin*, France, 1964, 115 mins, black-and-white)

Director: François Truffaut; *Production:* Les Films du Carrosse, SEDIF; *Director of Production:* Georges Charlot; *Screenplay:* François Truffaut, Jean-Louis Richard; *Editor:* Claudine Bouché; *Photography:* Raoul Coutard; *Music:* Georges Delerue

Principal Cast: Françoise Dorléac (Nicole), Jean Desailly (Pierre Lachenay), Nelly Benedetti (Franca), Daniel Ceccaldi (Clément), Jean Lanier (Michel), Paule Emanuele (Odile), Sabine Haudepin (Sabine), Laurence Badie

(Ingrid), Gérard Poirot (Franck), Georges de Givray (Nicole's father)

Danish Oscar 'Bodil', for Best European Film.

On a trip to Lisbon, Pierre Lachenay, aged 43, the married publisher of a literary magazine in Paris, has a brief affair with a young air hostess, Nicole. Back in Paris he contacts her again, and they meet several times in hotels, but find it squalid. He takes the opportunity of a lecture in Reims to spend a few days with her in the country, but the need for secrecy, which keeps Nicole hanging about while he fulfils his commitments, means that the weekend is not successful. His wife begins to suspect his infidelity and, faced by her jealous rage, he leaves her, determined to marry Nicole. She, however, is not interested in marriage and walks out. Pierre tries to ring his wife, but she, having found proof of his fidelity, has already left for the restaurant where she knows he will be and where she shoots him dead.

> I realized pretty quickly that *La Peau Douce* would be a failure, as soon as I'd finished the mixing. I looked at the film very lucidly, as if somebody else had made it, and I saw that it was depressing, that it was a film which 'went downwards'. I understood then that it would be disagreeable to watch. (Truffaut)

FAHRENHEIT 451 (Great Britain, 1966, 113 mins, Technicolor)

Director: François Truffaut; *Producer:* Lewis M. Allen for Vineyard Films Ltd; *Screenplay:* François Truffaut and Jean-Louis Richard, with additional dialogue by David Rudkin and Helen Scott, from the novel by Ray Bradbury; *Editor:* Thom Noble; *Photography:* Nicolas Roeg; *Design:* Syd Cain, Tony Walton; *Music:* Bernard Herrmann

Principal Cast: Julie Christie (Linda

Montag/Clarissa), Oskar Werner (Montag), Cyril Cusack (the Captain), Anton Diffring (Fabian), Jeremy Spencer (the man with the apple), Anne Bell (Doris), Caroline Hunt (Helen), Gillian Lewis (TV announcer), Anna Palk (Jackie), Roma Milne (neighbour), Bee Duffel (the book woman)

Montag is a fireman in a society of the future where his job is to seek out and burn books. He wins a recommendation for promotion, to the delight of his wife, Linda, who wants a new giant television screen for their living-room. When Montag meets Clarissa, a young schoolteacher who bears a strong resemblance to his wife, doubts about his job begin to form in his mind and are strengthened when his wife almost kills herself accidentally with a drug overdose. The next day he brings a book home instead of burning it. Soon his house is full of hidden books, and his dissatisfaction with his work is increased when Clarissa is sacked as a teacher and an old woman who refuses to leave her books is burnt alive with them. After an outburst when he insists on reading from *David Copperfield* to his wife's guests, he decides to leave the Fire Service. His final mission is to his own house: Linda has denounced him. Montag turns his flame-thrower on his colleagues, escapes from the city and finds the forest hideout of the 'book people', who save books by committing them to memory, and where he finds Clarissa. Montag starts memorizing the tales of Edgar Allan Poe.

We should have two good copies ready for Venice and that will be the end of this adventure in which I have gained a lot of white hairs and lost many more. . . . I don't yet know whether the result will give the impression of a normal film made by a lunatic or a lunatic film made by a normal person, but I am convinced that in writing a book or making a film we are abnormal people addressing normal people. Sometimes our folly is accepted, sometimes it is rejected. (Truffaut, from *Journal de Fahrenheit 451*, Seghers, 1974)

LA MARIÉE ÉTAIT EN NOIR
(US/UK: *The Bride Wore Black*, France, 1967, 105 mins, Eastmancolor)

Director: François Truffaut; *Production:* Les Films du Carrosse, Artistes Associés, Dino de Laurentiis; *Screenplay:* François Truffaut, Jean-Louis Richard, from the novel *The Bride Wore Black* by 'William Irish' (Cornell Woolrych); *Editor:* Claudine Bouché; *Photography:* Raoul Coutard; *Design:* Pierre Guffroy; *Music:* Bernard Herrmann

Principal Cast: Jeanne Moreau (Julie Kohler), Claude Rich (Bliss), Jean-Claude Brialy (Corey), Michel Bouquet (Coral), Michel Lonsdale (Morane), Charles Denner (Fergus), Daniel Boulanger (Delvaux), Serge Rousseau (David), Christophe Bruno (Cookie), Alexandra Stewart (Mlle Becker), Jacques Robiolles (Charlie), Luce Fabiole (Julie's mother), Sylvie Delannoy (Mme Morane)

Edgar Poe Prize (USA); Hollywood Foreign Press Award.

After her bridegroom has been shot dead on the church steps at their wedding, Julie Kohler sets out to find and kill the five men accidentally responsible for his death. She first finds Bliss, and at his engagement party, after discouraging the advances of his friend Corey, pushes Bliss to his death from the balcony of his apartment. Next she travels to a mountain village where she entrances a lonely, timid bank clerk, Robert Coral, before poisoning him. She gains admission to the house of René Morane, an aspiring politician, by posing as a teacher at his son's school, then traps and seals Morane in a cupboard, leaving him to suffocate. When his arrest for fraud saves her next victim, a shady car dealer named Delvaux, she moves on to the fifth, an artist called Fergus. She agrees to model for him as Diana the Huntress, but is disturbed to find that he is a friend of Corey, and further distressed when Fergus declares his love for her. Corey find Fergus killed by an arrow from Diana's bow. Julie allows Corey to turn her in to the police, but while helping in the prison kitchen she steals a knife which she uses to stab Delvaux and complete her revenge.

> I don't like *The Bride* too much. It wasn't very successful. And it wasn't a very good role for Jeanne Moreau – she's best when she expresses herself, when she talks, and here her role was static. She was a statue. . . . She was miscast. Also, the photography wasn't mysterious. It was too clear for a film of mystery. After this film, I decided to no longer show the sun in my pictures – neither the sun nor the sky. (Truffaut)

BAISERS VOLÉS (US/UK: *Stolen Kisses*, France, 1968, 90 mins, Eastmancolor)

Director: François Truffaut; *Production:* Les Films du Carrosse, Artistes Associés; *Executive Producer:* Marcel Berbert, assisted by Claude Miller; *Screenplay:* François Truffaut, Claude de Givray, Bernard Revon; *Editor:* Agnès Guillemot; *Photography:* Denys Clerval; *Design:* Claude Pignot; *Music:* Antoine Duhamel; song 'Que reste-t-il de nos amours', written and sung by Charles Trenet

Principal Cast: Jean-Pierre Léaud (Antoine Doinel), Claude Jade (Christine), Daniel Ceccaldi (Monsieur Darbon), Claire Duhamel (Mme Darbon), Delphine Seyrig (Fabienne Tabard), Michel Lonsdale (Monsieur Tabard), André Falcon (Monsieur Blady), Harry Max (Monsieur Henri), Catherine Lutz (Mme Catherine), Christine Pellé (secretary of the Blady agency), Marie-France Pisier (Colette Tazzi), Jean-François Adam (Albert Tazzi), Serge Rousseau (the mysterious stranger)

Grand Prix du Cinéma Français; Prix Méliès; Prix Fémina (Belgium), 1969; Prix Louis Delluc, 1969; British Film Institute Award, Best Foreign Film; Hollywood Foreign Press Association Award.

Dedicated to Henri Langlois.

Antoine Doinel, dishonourably discharged from the army, pays a quick visit to a prostitute before calling on his girlfriend, Christine Darbon. Christine's father finds him a job as night porter at a small hotel, but he is dismissed after being tricked by a private detective, Monsieur Henri, into interrupting an adulterous tryst between two of the hotel's guests. Henri finds Antoine work at the Blady Detective Agency, where he proves to be an incompetent sleuth. He is assigned to the case of Tabard, a shoe-store proprietor who wants to know why he is universally detested, and is planted in the shoe-store as a storeboy. Soon he is romantically and embarassingly in love with Tabard's beautiful wife, Fabienne, to whom (inspired by a Balzac novel) he writes a passionate letter of farewell. Fabienne, however, appears at Antoine's apartment, proposing that they should make love once before parting forever. Antoine agrees but, forced to admit the truth to Blady, loses his job. Some time later, Christine learns that Antoine is working as a television repair man. She summons him to mend her television and spends the night with him, which she had previously refused to do. Antoine and Christine get engaged.

> In my previous films I always started with a scenario made up of comic elements and serious elements. . . . My ideal would be to have as much gaiety as sadness, but I noticed that

. . . my films, in general, turned out sadder than had been anticipated. . . . This idea influenced *Stolen Kisses*: the scenario was purely comic and the more serious elements arose during the filming, so that we arrived at this 50/50 mixture that I had been seeking for a long time. (Truffaut)

LA SIRÈNE DU MISSISSIPPI (US: *Mississippi Mermaid*, France, 1969, 120 mins, Eastmancolor, Dyaliscope)

Director: François Truffaut; *Production:* Les Films du Carrosse, Artistes Associés, Produzioni Associate Delphos; *Executive Producer:* Marcel Berbert; *Director of Production:* Claude Miller; *Screenplay:* François Truffaut, from the novel *Waltz Into Darkness* by 'William Irish' (Cornell Woolrych); *Editor:* Agnès Guillemot; *Photography:* Denys Clerval; *Design:* Claude Pignot; *Music:* Antoine Duhamel

Principal Cast: Catherine Deneuve (Marion), Jean-Paul Belmondo (Louis Mahé), Michel Bouquet (Comolli), Nelly Borgeaud (Berthe Roussel), Marcel Berbert (Jardine), Roland Thénot (Richard)

Dedicated to Jean Renoir.

Meeting the steamer *Mississippi* to welcome Julie Roussel, the woman he has arranged to marry solely by letter, Louis Mahé, the wealthy owner of a cigarette factory on Réunion, is surprised when the girl who presents herself is not at all like the Julie he has been expecting. Nevertheless, he falls in love with and marries her. Inconsistencies in her behaviour and a letter from her sister Berthe claiming that she has not heard from Julie lead to the discovery that Julie has disappeared with most of his bank account. Berthe Roussel arrives, and she and Louis engage a private detective, Comolli. Louis leaves for Marseilles, where he accidentally discovers Julie working in a night-club. He confronts her, but cannot go through with his intention of killing her. Julie, whose real name is Marion, reveals how she and her accomplice, Richard, murdered the real Julie on board the *Mississippi*, how she genuinely loves Louis, and how Richard has absconded with all the money. Tenuously reconciled, they set up home in Aix, but Comolli has traced Julie/Marion this far, and Louis is forced to shoot him. Louis and Marion flee to Lyon, and Louis sells his factory, but Comolli's body is discovered, and they are forced to flee from Lyon, leaving most of the money behind, and to take shelter in a deserted cabin in the Alps. There Marion begins to poison Louis, until he finds out and shames her by declaring his love and his acceptance of her treachery. Reconciled again, they leave together through the snow.

The love scenes between Catherine and Belmondo weren't bad, but the thriller element wasn't very good. It was too light'. (Truffaut)

L'ENFANT SAUVAGE (US/UK: *The Wild Child*, France, 1970, 85 mins, black-and-white)

Director: François Truffaut; *Production:* Les Films du Carrosse, Artistes Associés; *Executive Producer:* Marcel Berbert; *Director of Production:* Claude Miller; *Screenplay:* François Truffaut, Jean Gruault, based on *Mémoire et Rapport sur Victor de l'Aveyron* by Jean Itard [1806]; *Editor:* Agnès Guillemot; *Photography:* Nestor Almendros; *Design:* Jean Mandaroux; *Music:* Antonio Vivaldi; *Musical Director:* Antoine Duhamel

Principal Cast: Jean-Pierre Cargol (Victor), François Truffaut (Jean Itard), Françoise Seigner (Mme Guérin), Jean Dasté (Philippe Pinel), Paul Villé (Rémy), Pierre Fabre (male nurse), Claude Miller (M Lémeri), Annie Miller (Mme Lémeri)

Golden Palm, Valladolid Festival; Christopher Award; Prix Fémina (Belgium).

Dedicated to Jean-Pierre Léaud.

In the Aveyron in 1797 local villagers trap a child who has been living wild in the woods. After being briefly imprisoned he is sent, at the request of doctor Jean Itard, to the Institute for Deaf Mutes in Paris. Examination reveals that the child is not deaf, but has numerous scars on his body caused by fights with animals and possibly his parents' attempt to slit his throat before abandoning him in the forest. At the Institute the boy is exhibited as a freak and tormented by the other children. Professor Pinel recommends his transfer to the insane asylum at Bicêtre, but Itard, anxious to prove that the child's problems are not congenital, obtains custody of him and installs him in his country house, under the care of his housekeeper, Madame Guérin. They set about slowly awakening the boy's sensibilities and intelligence: he learns to wear clothes, sleep in a bed, observe mealtime rituals and respond to the name of Victor. He learns to recognize and spell certain words, and Itard persuades the authorities to let him continue his experiment. Victor progresses, but continues to show signs of a violent temper. Itard deliberately inflicts an unjust punishment on him and concludes from his reaction that he is now a moral as well as a physical being. Later, Victor runs away, but returns after one night spent outdoors. His education continues.

The film's great strength is that it neither justifies nor challenges Itard's fundamental assumption that it is better to be a thinking man than a wild animal. The process by which he educates Victor to the estate of manhood involves constant small cruelties for the sake of a greater kindness, and Truffaut leaves the audience free to pass their own judgement. . . . The resulting film is not just a loving, virtually documentary reconstruction of a real incident of an earlier age, but also an impassioned assertion of man's right to extend his capacities. (Jan Dawson, *Monthly Film Bulletin*)

The subject of this film corresponded to themes that interest me and I realize now that *The Wild Child* is related both to *Les 400 Coups* and *Fahrenheit 451*. In *Les 400 Coups* I showed a child who is not loved, who grows up without tenderness; in *Fahrenheit 451* it is a man who is deprived of books, that is of culture. Victor's 'lack' is even more radical, it is language. These three films, therefore, are based on a major frustration. Even in my other films I describe characters who are outside society; they do not reject society, society rejects them. (Truffaut)

Up to *The Wild Child*, whenever there were children in my films I identified with them, but here for the first time I identified with an adult, the father, so that after the montage I dedicated the film to Jean-Pierre Léaud. (Truffaut)

DOMICILE CONJUGAL (US/UK: *Bed and Board*, France, 1970, 97 mins, Eastmancolor)

Director: François Truffaut; *Production:* Les Films du Carrosse, Valoria Films, Fida Cinematografica; *Executive Producer:* Marcel Berbert; *Director of Production*: Claude Miller; *Screenplay:* François Truffaut, Claude de Givray, Bernard Revon; *Editor:* Agnès Guillemot; *Photography:* Nestor Almendros; *Design:* Jean Mandaroux; *Music:* Antoine Duhamel

Principal Cast: Jean-Pierre Léaud (Antoine Doinel), Claude Jade (Christine), Daniel Ceccaldi (Lucien Darbon), Claire Duhamel (Mme Darbon), Mlle Hiroko (Kyoko), Barbara Laage (Monique), Sylvana Blasi (the tenor's wife), Daniel Boulanger (the tenor), Claude Véga (the strangler), Bill Kearns (American boss)

Antoine Doinel and Christine, now married, live in an apartment overlooking a bustling Paris courtyard. He has a job of sorts dyeing flowers for a local florist; she gives violin lessons to children. After a disaster in an attempt to find the perfect red dye Antoine fortuitously finds work with an American construction company, his job being to steer toy boats around a model harbour. The Doinels have a son, Alphonse. Antoine drifts into an affair with Kyoko, a beautiful Japanese girl, and when Christine discovers this she throws him out. But the doting father Antoine continues to visit his son and tells Christine of his growing boredom with his inscrutable oriental beauty. One evening in the course of an interminable restaurant meal with Kyoko, he telephones Christine three times, and Kyoko finally leaves. One year later, Antoine and Christine are once again happily married.

> I think I have now finished with Doinel for several reasons. First because there would from now on be too big a gap between him and Jean-Pierre, or between him and me; we would need to give him an ambition, a goal, which he doesn't have at the moment because it's not his nature. . . . Also and especially because I think I've already made the sequels to *Bed and Board*, even if in a different style, in my other films, and not only *Silken Skin*. . . . My concern now is to find new directions in which to work with Jean-Pierre, perhaps a period picture in which I could put him in costume and get him away from Doinel. (Truffaut)

LES DEUX ANGLAISES (Original release title: *Les Deux Anglaises et le*

Continent, UK: *Anne and Muriel*, France, 1971 [full version, 1985], original release version, 118 mins; full version, 132 mins, Eastmancolor)

Director: François Truffaut; *Production:* Les Films du Carrosse, Cinetel; *Executive Producer:* Marcel Berbert; *Director of Production:* Claude Miller; *Screenplay:* François Truffaut, Jean Gruault, from the novel *Les Deux Anglaises et le Continent* by Henri-Pierre Roché; *Editor:* Yann Dedet; *Photography:* Nestor Almendros; *Design:* Michel de Broin; *Music:* Georges Delerue

Principal Cast: Jean-Pierre Léaud (Claude Roc), Kika Markham (Anne), Stacey Tendeter (Muriel), Sylvia Marriott (Mrs Brown), Marie Mansart (Claire Roc), Philippe Léotard (Diurka), Irène Tunc (Ruta), Annie Miller (Mme de Montferrand), Jeanne Lobre (concierge), Marie Irakane (maid), Mark Peterson (Mr Flint), commentary spoken by François Truffaut

In Paris in 1899 Mme Roc, a widow and possessive mother, is visited by Anne Brown, the daughter of an old friend, also widowed. Her son Claude, an aspiring writer, escorts Anne, an aspiring sculptor, around art museums and, enchanted with her and her eulogies of her younger sister Muriel, accepts an invitation to stay in the Browns' cottage on the Welsh coast. Claude is fascinated by Muriel's moodiness and enjoys an easy relationship with both sisters until Mrs Brown, suspecting an affair between Claude and Muriel, banishes him to the home of her neighbour, Mr Flint. Claude proposes marriage to Muriel, but, faced with her mother's objections, they agree to a year's separation as a test of their love. After six months Claude breaks the engagement, telling Muriel that he has several mistresses. Later, Anne returns to Paris to pursue her career, loses her virginity to Claude, now a minor critic and art dealer, and eventually enjoys a passionate affair with him before leaving him to spend a year in Persia with Diurka, an art book publisher. Shortly after Mme Roc's death, Anne comes to Paris with Muriel. Convinced that Claude and Muriel are in love, she decides to sacrifice her own feelings, but her confession provokes a nervous collapse in the delicate Muriel, and both sisters return to Wales. In 1905 Claude publishes his first novel, *Jérôme and Julien*. He learns from Diurka, now his publisher, that Anne had died from tuberculosis and that Muriel will be passing through France on her way to a teaching post in Brussels. Muriel yields her virginity to him in a night of passionate love-making, but refuses to see him again. Fifteen years later, Muriel is married to an English schoolteacher, while Claude is alone and ageing fast.

> The most embarassing question usually posed to a director is 'What were you trying to do?'. As far as *Les Deux Anglaises* is concerned the answer came to me suddenly during the mixing, watching the celluloid going backwards and forwards, I understood that I had wanted to squeeze love like a lemon. . . . I felt the need to go further than one usually goes in the description of the emotions of love; sometimes there is in love a real violence of feelings, that's what I wanted to film. . . . To sum up in one sentence, I tried to make not a film about physical love, but a physical film about love. (Truffaut)

UNE BELLE FILLE COMME MOI

(US: *Such a Gorgeous Kid Like Me*; UK: *A Gorgeous Kid Like Me*, France, 1972, 98 mins, Eastmancolor, Panavision)

Director: François Truffaut; *Production:* Les Films du Carrosse, Columbia; *Executive Producer:* Marcel Berbert; *Director of Production:* Claude Miller;

Screenplay: François Truffaut, Jean-Loup Dabadie, from the novel *Such a Gorgeous Kid Like Me* by Henry Farrell; *Editor:* Yann Dedet; *Photography:* Pierre-William Glenn; *Design:* Jean-Pierre Kohut-Svelko; *Music:* Georges Delerue

Principal Cast: Bernadette Lafont (Camille Bliss), Claude Brasseur (Murène), Charles Denner (Arthur), Guy Marchand (Sam Golden), André Dussollier (Stanislas Prévine), Philippe Léotard (Clovis Bliss), Anne Kreis (Hélène), Gilberte Géniat (Isobel Bliss), Danièle Girard (Florence Golden), Martine Ferrière (prison secretary), Michel Delahaye (Marchal)

Stanislas Prévine, a naive sociologist researching a book on criminal women, interviews Camille Bliss, who tells him her life story. Suspected of murdering her father, she progresses from orphanage to reform school. Escaping, she takes up with Clovis Bliss, who conceals her from his tyrannical mother, but she forces him into marriage by claiming to be pregnant. After failing in an attempt to kill Mme Bliss, Camille steals her money and forces a reluctant Clovis to go with her to Paris. Their car breaks down outside a night-club, where Camille is engaged as a waitress and soon begins an affair with the singer Sam Golden. Clovis's jealousy lands him in hospital after a near fatal accident, and Camille is soon sharing her favours with Murène, a seedy lawyer who offers to fix an insurance claim for her. Meanwhile she has also inspired the devotion of Arthur, a puritanical rodent exterminator, who provides her with money and guiltily becomes her lover. Double-crossed by Murène, Camille tries to kill him and Clovis, but they are rescued by Arthur who, realizing that Camille has lied to him, orders her to join him in a suicide pact. He jumps from a church tower, but Camille is arrested for his murder. Stanislas, having heard all this, proves Camille's innocence of Arthur's murder, but after spending the night with her he finds Clovis dead and himself arrested for murder. He later learns from the TV that his lawyer, Marchal, is now Camille's 'good friend' and managing her singing career.

I like the film, but nobody saw it. It has a bad reputation: there are people who didn't understand why I made it. It's a feminist film, but unconventionally so. The heroine does only forbidden, dishonest things, but in fact she fights for her survival – because she only sees around her men who are also dishonest and who want to take advantage. . . . People in France didn't understand it and intellectuals detested it, because they probably felt I was mocking them: the man who tapes her and is in love with her. . . . But couldn't it have been myself I was ridiculing? I actually felt I depicted the Dussollier character affectionately, as timid. . . . She's stronger because she fights for her life. (Truffaut)

LA NUIT AMÉRICAINE (US/UK: *Day For Night*, France, 1973, 115 mins, Eastmancolor, Panavision)

Director: François Truffaut; *Production:* Les Films du Carrosse, PECF (Paris), PIC (Rome); *Executive Producer:* Marcel Berbert; *Screenplay:* François Truffaut, Jean-Louis Richard, Suzanne Schiffman; *Editor:* Yann Dedet; *Photography:* Pierre-William Glenn; *Design:* Damien Lanfranchi; *Music:* Georges Delerue

Principal Cast: Jacqueline Bisset (Julie Baker), Valentina Cortese (Séverine), Alexandra Stewart (Stacey), Jean-Pierre Aumont (Alexandre), Jean-Pierre Léaud (Alphonse), François Truffaut (Ferrand), Jean Champion (Bertrand), Nathalie Baye (Joëlle), Dani (Liliane), Bernard Menez (Bernard), Nike Arrighi (Odile), Gaston

Lajoie), Maurice Séveno (TV reporter), David Markham (Dr Nelson)

Oscar, Best Foreign Film, 1973.

Dedicated to Lillian and Dorothy Gish.

The cast and crew of the film *Je vous présente Paméla* gather at the Victorine studio in Nice: the actor Alphonse gets his girlfriend Liliane a job as a script-girl; Séverine, who plays Alphonse's mother in the film, is aghast that the man cast as her lover, Alexandre, is a former lover still able to land romantic roles; and the unit speculate about the mysterious 'lover' for whom Alexandre is frequently waiting at the airport. Problems accumulate for the director, Ferrand: the labs ruin a crowd scene; Séverine, increasingly resorting to drink, bungles a scene; another actress, Stacey, turns out to be pregnant; Alphonse is obsessed by jealousy about Liliane. The Hollywood actress who is to play Pamela, Julie Baker, recovering from a nervous breakdown, arrives with her new husband, Dr Michael Nelson. Alexandre finally returns from the airport with a young man, Christian. Liliane deserts Alphonse and runs off with an English stuntman. Alphonse threatens to quit movies altogether: Julie spends the night with him, and he impulsively tells Dr Nelson. Julie becomes distraught, Alphonse disappears, and shooting can only resume when Julie and Dr Nelson are reconciled and Alphonse returns repentant. Alexandre is killed in a car crash, necessitating hurried changes and 'simplification' in the script. Amidst a flurry of leavetaking, new plans and pairings, the unit disbands.

Of all meditations by film-makers on film-making *Day For Night* is certainly very modest about the director as superstar, and the production of *Meet Pamela* offers no more riveting a display of artistic temperament than an actress fluffing her lines. . . . Truffaut, in fact, seems to have cast himself as a mere super-artisan all the better to commemorate the work of his fellow craftsmen and the tools of their trade. The problems of filming on *Meet Pamela* are eminently practical. . . . while the problems of creation are always at a remove, and viewed romantically, nostalgically. (Richard Combs, *Monthly Film Bulletin*)

Truffaut shows us what the cinema as a profession is all about and why he loves it. . . . (He) has continued on his own account Jean Renoir's meditations on performance: he has made his *Carrosse d'Or*. With in addition a multitude of Lubitsch touches. It is amusing, truthful and moving. The intelligence of the heart is triumphant. (Jean-Louis Bory, *Le Nouvel Observateur*)

Through the young actor played by Jean-Pierre Léaud, I am pondering over a question which has been worrying me for 30 years: is the cinema more important than real life? This is perhaps no more intelligent than asking: 'Do you prefer your mother or your father?' But I have been thinking about the cinema so many hours every day and for so many years that I can't stop myself from putting life and films in competition with each other. (Truffaut)

L'HISTOIRE D'ADÈLE H (US/UK: *The Story of Adèle H*, France, 1975, 110 mins, Eastmancolor, Panavision)

Director: François Truffaut; *Production:* Les Films du Carrosse, Artistes Associés; *Directors of Production:* Marcel Berbert, Claude Miller; *Screenplay:* François Truffaut, Jean Gruault, based on *Le Journal d'Adèle Hugo*, ed. Frances Vernor Guille; *Editor:* Yann Dedet; *Photography:* Nestor Almendros; *Design:* Jean-Pierre Kohut-Svelko; *Music:* Maurice Jaubert

Principal Cast: Isabelle Adjani (Adèle

Hugo), Bruce Robinson (Lt Pinson), Sylvia Marriott (Mrs Saunders), Reuben Dory (Mr Saunders), Joseph Blatchley (Whistler, the bookseller), Mr White (the colonel), Carl Hathwell (Pinson's orderly), Ivry Gitlis (the hypnotist), Sir Cecil de Sausmarez (Maître Lenoir, notary), Sir Raymond Falla (Judge Johnstone), Roger Martin (Dr Murdock), Madame Louise (Mme Baa). Most of the cast is composed of amateurs, inhabitants of Guernsey and the island of Gorée, Senegal.

Grand Prix du Cinéma, Français, 1975; New York Film Critics Society Awards: Best Original Screenplay, Best Actress (Isabelle Adjani).

1863. Adèle, younger daughter of Victor Hugo, disembarks in Halifax, Nova Scotia, taking lodgings under an assumed name. She is tracking Lt Albert Pinson, an English officer she fell in love with in Guernsey, where her father is a political exile. Pinson, who may once have loved her but was not viewed favourably as a prospective son-in-law, makes it clear that he has no desire to marry her. In failing health and haunted by memories of her sister Léopoldine's death in a boating accident, Adèle showers Pinson with love letters, lends him money for his gambling debts, and spies on him. With scandal on the point of breaking out, Adèle finally gets her father's permission to marry Pinson and gives herself to him, hoping that he could love her despite his continued refusal to marry her. When she writes home saying she is married, an announcement in the Guernsey papers results in an embarassing interview for Pinson with his commanding officer. Despite her mother being ill, Adèle refuses to return home while Pinson is still in Halifax. She sends Pinson a whore as a present; considers using a hypnotist to change his feelings; breaks up his engagement by telling his fiancée's father that she is pregnant; and has to move into a doss-house when her money runs out. Her father sends her the fare home, but she uses it to follow Pinson to his new posting in Barbados. There, now completely insane, she is cared for by the kindly Madame Baa and ignores Pinson when he seeks her out. She returns home accompanied by Madame Baa.

If I have to sum up in seven points what attracts me in the story of Adèle Hugo, these would be:
1. This girl is alone throughout the story.
2. She is the daughter of the most famous man in the world.
3. This man is talked about but never seen.
4. Adèle lives under false identities.
5. Inspired by an *idée fixe*, she pursues an unattainable goal.
6. All Adèle's words, all her actions, are related to her *idée fixe*.
7. Even if she is fighting a losing battle, Adèle is continuously active and inventive.
Let me say that, being incapable of making films 'against', I go on making films 'for', and that I love with the same love Antoine Doinel, Catherine, Montag, Julie, Muriel Brown, Victor de l'Aveyron and Adèle H. (Truffaut)

L'ARGENT DE POCHE (US/UK: *Small Change*, France, 1976, 104 mins, Eastmancolor)

Director: François Truffaut; *Production:* Les Films du Carrosse, Artistes Associés; *Directors of Production:* Marcel Berbert, Roland Thénot; *Screenplay:* François Truffaut, Suzanne Schiffman; *Editor:* Yann Dedet; *Photography:* Pierre-William Glenn; *Design:* Jean-Pierre Kohut-Svelko; *Music:* Maurice Jaubert; Song 'Les enfants s'ennuient le dimanche', written and sung by Charles Trenet

Principal Cast: Children: Geory Desmouceaux (Patrick Desmouceaux), Bruno Staab (Bruno Rouillard), Philippe Goldmann (Julien Leclou), Corinne Boucart (Corinne), Eva Truffaut (Patricia), Sylvie Grézel (Sylvie), Laurent Devlaeminck (Laurent Riffle), Franck Deluca (Franck Deluca), Claudio Deluca (Mathieu Deluca), Richard Golfier (Richard Golfier), Pascale Bruchon (Martine), Laura Truffaut (Madeleine Doinel), Sébastien Marc (Oscar), and Grégory; Adults: Jean-François Stévenin (Jean-François Richet), Virginie Thévenet (Lydie Richet), Chantal Mercier (Mlle Petit), Nico Félix (Nico), Tania Torrens (Mme Riffle), Francis Devlaeminck (M. Riffle), Jean-Marie Carayon (the commissioner, Sylvie's father), Kathie Carayon (Sylvie's mother), Christian Lentretien (M. Golfier), Marcel Berbert (headmaster), Roland Thénot (the bookseller), Christine Pellé (Mme Leclou), Jane Lobre (Julien's grandmother)

Episodes from the lives of a group of children in Thiers, a town at the geographical centre of France. During break at school Mathieu and Frank use binoculars to watch a woman undress in a nearby apartment. Patrick, who lives alone with a father confined to a wheelchair, has a crush on his best friend's mother, Mme Riffle, and presents her with a large bouquet of red roses, which unfortunately she assumes to be from his father. Two-year-old Grégory, left unattended in a tower-block apartment, crawls onto a window ledge and falls, only to survive miraculously unhurt. Julien Leclou arrives at school in mid-term, frequently appears bruised and battered and sleeps through class. When he is sent out of class one day as a punishment, he goes through the pockets of the coats hanging in the hall. On Sundays most of the children assemble in the local cinema. Patricia, forced to stay at home by her parents as a punishment for being argumentative, uses her father's loud hailer to draw attention to her plight and receives food parcels from sympathetic neighbours. Patrick and Bruno, an older friend, pick up a couple of girls and take them to the cinema, but Patrick is embarassed by Bruno's greater sexual know-how. A routine medical check just before the vacation reveals that Julien has been severely maltreated. His mother and aged grandmother are arrested. On the last day of school the teacher, M. Richet, delivers a lecture to the class which he hopes will help them to understand a case like Julien's. At summer camp a ruse by the other children enables Patrick to exchange a first kiss with his girlfriend.

> We wanted to create laughter, not at the expense of the children but 'with them', not even at the expense of the adults but 'with them', hence the attempt at a delicate balance between seriousness and lightness. (Truffaut)

> Many people have complained about the niceness of the film; I think it was necessary because the children wandered around the camera, wanted to know how it worked; they were very interested in the mechanics of it. . . . I showed them the rushes at the local cinema: I wasn't going to barricade the doors to keep them out! . . . So little by little they entered so far into the film that I felt it was becoming their film, and that I was making it for them. (Truffaut)

L'HOMME QUI AIMAIT LES FEMMES (US/UK: *The Man Who Love Women*, France, 1977, 115 mins, Eastmancolor)

Director: François Truffaut; *Production:* Les Films du Carrosse, Artistes Associés; *Executive Producer:* Marcel Berbert; *Screenplay:* François Truffaut, Michel Fermaud, Suzanne Schiffman; *Editor:*

Martine Barraqué-Curie; *Photography:* Nestor Almendros; *Design:* Jean-Pierre Kohut-Svelko; *Music:* Maurice Jaubert

Principal Cast: Charles Denner (Bertrand Morane), Brigitte Fossey (Geneviève Bigey), Nelly Borgeaud (Delphine Grezel), Geneviève Fontanel (Hélène), Nathalie Baye (Martine Desdoits), Sabine Glaser (Bernadette), Valérie Bonnier (Fabienne), Martine Chassaing (Denise), Roselyne Puyo (Nicole), Anna Perrier (Uta), Monique Dury (Mme Duteil), Nella Barbier (Liliane), Fréderique Jamet (Juliette), Marie-Jeanne Montfajon (Christiane, Bertrand's mother), Leslie Caron (Véra), Jean Dasté (Dr Bicard), Roger Leenhardt (M. Bétany)

Bertrand Morane, an engineer living in Montpellier, spends his leisure in an obsessive pursuit of women. He goes to great lengths to trace a woman whose legs he has admired, finally doing so through her car. He traces the car-owner, Martine, but finds that the woman he had seen was her cousin, who has now returned to Canada. He is friends with Hélène, the manageress of a dress shop, but she rejects his advances because she only likes men younger than herself. Bertrand decides to write his memoirs, spurred on by memories of his amorous mother and his own early sexual experiences. The women involved include Liliane, for whom he obtained a job at his factory and with whom he enjoys a platonic friendship, and Delphine, a married woman whose pleasure lies in making love in potentially hazardous circumstances, and who finally shoots and wounds her husband and goes to jail. Bertrand's manuscript is accepted by the publishing house, Bétany, thanks to Geneviève, one of the editors. In Paris, Bertrand has a chance encounter with Véra, with whom he once had an affair, the end of which has strongly marked them both. Bertrand spends a weekend in the country with Geneviève while his book is being published, but at Christmas, running across a road after Denise, with whom he works but who he has hitherto ignored, he is hit by a car and taken to hospital. He is forbidden to move, but, irresistably attracted by his nurse's legs, leans out of bed and breaks his blood-transfusion tube. His funeral draws a large crowd of mourners, all women, and his book is published.

If one phrase could serve as the common denominator for Bertrand's love affairs it would be this, from Bruno Bettelheim's *The Empty Fortress*: 'It would appear that Joey never had any success with his mother'. (Truffaut)

I was working on something mythical. The myth must be respected. The death scene in the hospital, looking at the nurse's legs, was told by the character played by Daniel Boulanger in *Shoot the Pianist*, evoking the death of his father. Here it was visualized. His death is obviously not a punishment. It's a question of logic. (Truffaut)

LA CHAMBRE VERTE (US/UK: *The Green Room*, France, 1978, 94 mins, Eastmancolor)

Director: François Truffaut; *Production:* Les Films du Carrosse, Artistes Associés; *Director of Production:* Roland Thénot; *Executive Producer:* Marcel Berbert; *Screenplay:* François Truffaut, Jean Gruault, on themes from short stories by Henry James, 'The Altar of the Dead', 'The Way It Came', and 'The Beast in the Jungle'; *Editor:* Martine Barraqué; *Photography:* Nestor Almendros; *Design:* Jean-Pierre Kohut-Svelko; *Music:* Maurice Jaubert

Principal Cast: François Truffaut (Julien Davenne), Nathalie Baye (Cécilia Mandel), Jean Dasté (Bernard Humbert), Jean-Pierre Moulin (Gérard Mazet), Antoine Vitez (the bishop's secretary), Jane Lobre (Mme Rambaud), Patrick Maléon (Georges), Jean-Pierre Ducos (priest), Annie Miller (Geneviève Mazet), Marie Jaoul (Yvonne Mazet), Monique Dury (Monique)

Julien Davenne, a journalist on a local paper in eastern France shortly after the First World War, has set up a 'green room', a shrine to the memory of his wife, Julie, who died shortly after their marriage, which no one is allowed to enter and where he communes with the dead woman. The other members of his household are his deaf-mute nephew and the child's governess, Mme Rambaud. Julien tries to persuade his friend, Gérard Mazet, who is contemplating suicide after his wife's death, that the preservation of her memory is sufficient reason to go on living. Searching for souvenirs linked to Julie, Julien attends an auction of her family's belongings where Cécilia Mandel, a young assistant, agrees to help him find a ring of Julie's. Later, at the newspaper office, Julien avoids Mazet, who has come to introduce him to his second wife, and confesses to Cécilia, who seems to share his desire to preserve the memory of the dead, that he cannot forgive Mazet's decision to remarry. Julien commissions a life-size model of Julie from a local artisan, but smashes it in horror at its lifeless waxiness. When a fire destroys the green room, Julien decides to transform a disused chapel in the church graveyard into a shrine for all 'his dead'. He confides in Cécilia, but becomes estranged from her when he discovers that she was the mistress of the late Paul Massigny, a local politician and once Julien's best friend before betraying him, and whose memory she wants to preserve in the chapel. Later, though gravely ill, Julien meets Cécilia at the chapel, now transformed into his shrine, and admits he has been ungenerous towards her and Massigny. In the bitterly cold weather Julien dies, and Cécilia lights a final candle for him.

François Truffaut's best films often show an individual pursuing an obsession to the very end: after the vengeance of *The Bride Wore Black*, the suicidal madness of *Adèle H*, and the desperate search of *The Man Who Loved Women*, *The Green Room* is the enclosed space of a ritual like no other: the cult of the dead. In its simplicity and purity, the film looks like a cinematic testament: there will be other Truffaut films, but shall we see any more intimate, more personal, more heartrending than this *Green Room*? (Michel Grisolia, *Le Nouvel Observateur*)

With each year that passes we cross out more names in our address books, and there comes a moment when we realize that we know more of the dead than the living.

This simple fact lies behind the screenplay of *The Green Room*, written by Jean Gruault and myself, and which combines themes from stories by Henry James with biographical elements concerning the writer's fidelity to the memory of his wife. . . .

The Green Room is a love story, like all the films Jean Gruault and I have written together. This time we are showing the struggle in our hearts between provisional feelings and definitive feelings. (Truffaut)

L'AMOUR EN FUITE (US/UK: *Love on the Run*, France, 1979, 94 mins, Eastmancolor and black-and-white)

Director: François Truffaut; *Production:* Les Films du Carrosse; *Director of Production:* Roland Thénot; *Executive Producer:* Marcel Berbert; *Screenplay:* François Truffaut, Marie-France Pisier, Jean Aurel, Suzanne Schiffman; *Editor:* Martine Barraqué; *Photography:* Nestor Almendros; *Design:* Jean-Pierre Kohut-Svelko; *Music:* Georges Delerue; song 'L'amour en fuite', by Laurent Voulzy, Alain Souchon, sung by Alain Souchon

Principal Cast: Jean-Pierre Léaud (Antoine Doinel), Marie-France Pisier (Colette), Claude Jade (Christine), Dani (Liliane), Dorothée (Sabine Barnerias), Daniel Mesguich (Xavier Barnerias), Julien Bertheau (M. Lucien), Rosy Varte (Colette's mother), Marie Henriau (divorce court judge), Jean-Pierre Ducos (Christine's lawyer), Pierre Dios (Maître Renard), Alain Ollivier (judge at Aix), Monique Dury (Mme Ida)

Antoine Doinel, now separated from his wife Christine, is passionately involved with Sabine. A call from Christine summons the forgetful Antoine to her lawyer for their divorce decree. Antoine puts his son Alphonse on a train for his holiday, breaking a date with Sabine, who is annoyed at not being invited to meet Alphonse. Colette, his adolescent passion who is now a lawyer, has spotted him at the court and bought his autobiographical novel from her boyfriend, the bookshop proprietor, Xavier. She now waves to him from another train, and Antoine impulsively leaps aboard. She is going to Aix-en-Provence to defend a child murderer, and, after swapping reminiscences, she upbraids Antoine for his egotism. He pulls the emergency brake and leaves the train, leaving behind a torn-up picture of Sabine. On the back, Colette discovers that Sabine's surname is the same as Xavier's and, supposing them to be married, she rushes back to Paris (her case is cancelled when her client attempts suicide) only to find that they are brother and sister. Antoine has little success in making up with Sabine. He meets M. Lucien, an ex-lover of his late mother, and with him visits her grave for the first time. Colette gets back together with Xavier and Antoine is reconciled with Sabine.

> I was very unhappy with *Love on the Run*. The editing was the only good thing about it. It was an experiment. I think a film should start as an experiment, but not end up as one. You don't have the impression that you've seen a real film when you walk out of the theatre in this case. Part of what I don't like about the film is that the character hasn't evolved normally – he was like a cartoon. In cartoons you don't age; how can Mickey Mouse grow old? Antoine Doinel is like Mickey. . . . so I had to stop. (Truffaut)

LE DERNIER MÉTRO (US/UK: *The Last Metro*, France, 1980, 128 mins [complete video version, 134 mins] Fujicolor)

Director: François Truffaut, *Production:* Les Films du Carrosse, Andrea Films, SEDIF, TF1; *Director of Production:* Jean-José Richer; *Screenplay:* François Truffaut, Suzanne Schiffman, Jean-Claude Grumberg; *Editor:* Martine Barraqué; *Photography:* Nestor Almendros; *Design:* Jean-Pierre Kohut-Svelko; *Music:* Georges Delerue

Principal Cast: Catherine Deneuve (Marion Steiner), Gérard Depardieu (Bernard Granger), Jean Poiret (Jean-Loup Cottins), Andrea Férreol (Arlette Guillaume), Heinz Bennent (Lucas Steiner), Paulette Dubost (Germaine Fabre), Sabine Haudepin (Nadine Marsac), Jean-Louis Richard (Daxiat), Maurice Risch (Raymond Boursier), Marcel Berbert (Merlin), Richard Bohringer (Gestapo man), Jean-Pierre Klein (Christian Léglise), Frank Pasquier (Jacquot), Rose Thierry (Jacquot's mother), Laszlo Szabo (Lieutenant Bergen)

Césars 1981: Best Film, Best Screenplay, Best Actor (Gérard Depardieu), Best Actress (Catherine Deneuve), Photography, Sound (Michel Laurent), Editing, Design, Music; Prix Jean Le Duc, Archange du Cinéma.

In occupied Paris, September 1942, the actor Bernard Granger joins the prestigious Théâtre Montmartre, which has been run by the famous actress, Marion Steiner, since the supposed flight of her husband Lucas, a Polish Jew. Unknown to all but Marion, however, Lucas is hiding in the cellar, still able to direct plays through Marion. He has prepared notes on a Norwegian play, *Disappearance*, to be directed by his colleague Jean-Loup Cottins, who has to curry favour with the hated collaborator critic Daxiat in order to secure clearance from the censor. During rehearsals Bernard (who is secretly in the Resistance) tries to seduce the reluctant stage designer, Arlette Guillaume, while steadily becoming more attracted to Marion. Lucas, meanwhile, vents his anger when he learns that the Germans have occupied the Free Zone, to which he had hoped to escape, but finds some consolation in being able to listen in on rehearsals and offer his advice through Marion. The play is attacked by Daxiat for its 'covert Jewishness', and Bernard assaults the critic in public. Horrified that he may have jeopardized Lucas's safety, Marion tells Bernard never to talk to her off-stage, though now, having discovered that Arlette is a lesbian, he is more in love with her than ever. Marion fights Daxiat's attempt to have the theatre taken away from her, while Lucas barely escapes discovery when the Gestapo search the theatre. Marion and Bernard become lovers after he confesses his Resistance connection and tells her he is leaving the company. As the tide of war turns, Lucas emerges from hiding and is united on stage with Marion and Bernard to great audience acclaim.

In writing, with Suzanne Schiffman,

the scenario of *The Last Metro*, my intention was to do for the theatre what I had done for the cinema in *Day For Night*: the chronicle of a troop at work in a context respecting the unities of place, time and action. (Truffaut)

Today in 1983, if I must analyze the good reception given to *The Last Metro*, I think that by enriching the screenplay with details that struck me during my childhood I gave the film an originality of vision which it would not have had it if had been conceived by someone older (who would have experienced the Occupation as an adult) or younger (born after the war). . . . *The Last Metro*, probably, is simply this: the theatre and the Occupation seen by a child. (Truffaut)

LA FEMME D'À CÔTÉ (US/UK: *The Woman Next Door*, France, 1981, 106 mins, Fujicolor)

Director: François Truffaut; *Production:* Les Films du Carrosse, TF1; *Director of Production:* Armand Barbault; *Screenplay:* François Truffaut, Suzanne Schiffman, Jean Aurel; *Editor:* Martine Barraqué; *Photography:* William Lubtchansky; *Design:* Jean-Pierre Kohut-Svelko; *Music:* Georges Delerue

Principal Cast: Gérard Depardieu (Bernard Coutray), Fanny Ardant (Mathilde Bauchard), Henri Garcin (Philippe Bauchard), Michèle Baumgartner (Arlette Coudray), Roger Van Hool (Roland Duguet), Véronique Silver (Odile Jouve), Philippe Morier-Genoud (the doctor), Olivier Becquaert (Thomas Coudray).

In a village near Grenoble, Mathilde and Philippe Bauchard move in next door to Bernard and Arlette Coudray. Unbeknownst to their spouses, eight years ago Mathilde and Bernard had a passionate affair. Bernard meets Mathilde by accident in a supermarket and,

following a friendly reconciliation, impulsively embraces her, causing her to faint. At Mme Jouve's tennis club, Mathilde meets Ronald, a homosexual publisher, and re-embarks on her career as a children's book illustrator. Later, at Bernard's instigation, the lovers resume their affair, regularly meeting in the same Grenoble hotel room. Bernard suggests they start their lives anew, but Mathilde demurs, and they make love for what she declares is the last time. Bernard, for a moment jealous of Ronald, tries with increasing desperation to rekindle Mathilde's passion for him. Finally, at a garden party given by the Bauchards he loses all self-control and publicly beats Mathilde. Arlette, who is pregnant with her second child, and Philippe both seem reconciled with their respective and now contrite partners. But later, while signing copies of her new book at the tennis club, Mathilde suddenly breaks down, is taken to hospital, and will not be comforted even when visited by Bernard. She is fascinated by the story of Mme Jouve, who 20 years ago tried to kill herself when her lover left her and is crippled as a result. After she recovers, the Bauchards move house. One night Bernard is awakened by the noise of the door in the Bauchards' old house banging. Entering the house he meets Mathilde, they make love, and she shoots first him and then herself.

After *The Last Metro*, which contained six or seven characters of equal importance, I wanted to discipline myself with a tighter story centred around a couple. I deliberately kept the spouses in the background, choosing instead the character of a confidante to set the story moving and pronounce its conclusion: 'Neither with you nor without you'. What is *The Woman Next Door* about? Love and, of course, thwarted love, without which there would be no story. The obstacle, here, between the two lovers is not the pressure of society, nor the presence of another, neither is it the difference between two temperaments, but on the contrary their resemblance to each other. They are both still in the state of excitement of 'all or nothing' which caused them to split up eight years earlier. (Truffaut)

The structure of *The Woman Next Door* had existed for some years. What stopped me from going on with it was the symmetry of the characters I had imagined. There were two couple: four characters. I think, rightly or wrongly, that a story should include an odd number of characters.

Then I remembered a woman I'd met 15 years earlier. She had told me her life story, in an old quarter of Nice, while I was looking for a dinner jacket to wear to see Charles Trenet at the Casino. Thus was born Madame Jouve, the fifth character of *The Woman Next Door*. (Truffaut)

VIVEMENT DIMANCHE! (US: *Confidentially Yours*, UK: *Finally Sunday!*, France, 1983, 111 mins, black-and-white)

Director: François Truffaut; *Production:* Les Films du Carrosse, Films A2, Soprofilms; *Director of Production:* Armand Barbault; *Screenplay:* François Truffaut, Suzanne Schiffman, Jean Aurel, from the novel *The Long Saturday Night* by Charles Williams; *Editor:* Martine Barraqué; *Photography:* Nestor Almendros; *Design:* Hilton McConnico; *Music:* Georges Delerue

Principal Cast: Fanny Ardant (Barbara Becker), Jean-Louis Trintignant (Julien Vercel), Philippe Laudenbach (Maître Clément), Caroline Sihol (Marie-Christine Vercel), Philippe Morier-Genoud (Superintendent Santelli), Xavier Saint-Macary (Bertrand Fabre), Jean-Pierre Kalfon (Jacques Massoulier), Anik Belaubre (cashier at the Eden), Jean-Louis Richard (Louison), Yann Dedet (Angel Face), Georges Koulouris (Lablache), Roland Thénot (Jambau), Pierre Gare (Inspector Poivert).

Julien Vercel, an estate agent in a small town in the south of France, becomes a prime suspect when a friend, Jacques Massoulier, is shot while hunting, but protests his innocence. Later Vercel's wife is also murdered, and an anonymous letter reveals that she was Massoulier's mistress. Vercel's secretary, Barbara Becker, who is secretly in love with him, investigates while he remains hidden at his agency. In Nice, she traces a man also interested in Mme Vercel's affairs to the Lablache Detective Agency. She and Lablache learn that Vercel's wife had been a prostitute, involved with a night-club, the Ange Rouge, whose owner, Louison, also runs a cinema and is involved in a network of vice and blackmail. Louison is murdered, as is the cinema's cashier, another former mistress of Massoulier's and writer of anonymous letters. After discovering a secret passage between the office of Maître Clément, Vercel's lawyer, and that of Mme Vercel, Barbara leads the police to Vercel's hiding place. This is a ruse to trap the real murderer, Clément, who is tricked into giving himself away and admits his guilt and his feelings about women over the telephone. Vercel and Barbara are free to marry.

Not only has the wheel come full circle, but the idea of *caméra stylo* – a cinema of personal expression – has asserted itself with a vengeance. One of the prime functions of a ballpoint, after all, is to doodle. And that, precisely, is what *Vivement Dimanche* is: a masterly doodle, executed with love, skill and flourish. (Nick Roddick, *Sight and Sound*)

There is an experimental side to *Vivement Dimanche*: to blend a thriller with a two-handed comedy. I wanted to see whether I could mix it all up in one film. And also to present Fanny Ardant, who has a romantic and lyrical image, as a comic heroine, a little like Katharine Hepburn. For this the character had to speak rapidly, intrude on other peoples' dialogue, she had to be consistently robust, very alive. . . . This is difficult, and I worked on this film for a long time, ten times longer than on *The Woman Next Door*. (Truffaut)

Notes

Chapter One

1 Claude Chabrol, *Et pourtant je tourne* . . . (Paris: Robert Laffont, 1976), p. 135.

Chapter Two

1 Gilles Cahoreau, *François Truffaut, 1932–1984* (Paris: Julliard, 1989), p. 22.
2 The quotations in this paragraph are taken from the introduction to Truffaut's *Les Films de ma vie* (Paris: Flammarion, 1975).
3 *Les Films de ma vie*, p. 14.
4 *Les Films de ma vie*, p. 366.
5 Quoted in Hervé Dalmais, *Truffaut* (Paris: Rivages, 1987), p. 17.
6 Quoted in Dalmais, p. 19.
7 Reprinted in François Truffaut, *Le Plaisir des yeux* (Paris: Flammarion, 1987), pp. 211–229.
8 Reprinted in *Le Plaisir des yeux*, pp. 234–249.
9 *Le Plaisir des yeux*, p. 249.
10 *Les Films de ma vie*, p. 16.
11 *Les Films de ma vie*, p. 325.
12 *Les Films de ma vie*, p. 137.
13 *Les Films de ma vie*, pp. 125–129. Truffaut was apparently unaware that the story of *Vera Cruz* had been largely invented during the making of the film!
14 *Les Films de ma vie*, p. 25.
15 Cahoreau, pp. 302–303.
16 *Le Plaisir des yeux*, p. 199.
17 *Le Plaisir des yeux*, pp. 93–94.
18 *Les Films de ma vie*, p. 27.
19 Jean Collet, *François Truffaut* (Paris: Lherminier, 1985), p. 73.
20 *Truffaut par Truffaut*, ed. Dominique Rabourdin (Paris: Chêne, 1985), p. 116.
21 Steven Spielberg, 'He Was the Movies', *Film Comment* (Jan–Feb 1985), pp. 40–41.
22 Cahoreau, p. 308.
23 *Le Monde* 4/5 November 1990.
24 Spielberg, 'He Was the Movies', p. 41.

Chapter Three

1 This is the title of an article in *Le Plaisir des yeux*, pp. 9–18.
2 *Truffaut par Truffaut*, p. 211.
3 *Le Plaisir des yeux*, p. 80.
4 *Truffaut par Truffaut*, p. 173.
5 *Le Roman de François Truffaut*, pp. 47–49.
6 Spielberg, 'He Was the Movies', p. 41.
7 Dalmais, *Truffaut*, p. 67.

Chapter Four

1 *Truffaut par Truffaut*, p. 34.
2 Dalmais, *Truffaut*, p. 140.
3 '1979 Année de l'enfance assassinée' in *Le Plaisir des yeux*, pp. 265–268.
4 *Truffaut par Truffaut*, p. 46.
5 Michel Cieutat, *Martin Scorsese* (Paris: Rivages, 1986), p. 63.
6 *Le Roman de François Truffaut*, pp. 123, 126–128, 130, 132; Spielberg, 'He Was the Movies', p. 41.

Bibliography

Books by Truffaut in English

Hitchcock (New York, Simon and Schuster, 1966; London, Secker and Warburg, 1968; 2nd 'definitive' edition, 1984).

The Films in My Life (New York, Simon and Schuster, 1978; London, Allen Lane, 1980; Harmondsworth, Penguin, 1982).

Letters, ed. Gilles Jacob and Claude de Givray; trans. Gilbert Adair (London, Faber and Faber, 1989).

Truffaut by Truffaut, ed. Dominique Rabourdin (London, 1990).

The second collection of Truffaut's articles *Le Plaisir des Yeux* (Paris, 1987) has yet to be translated into English.

Scripts in English

Jules and Jim, trans. Nicholas Fry (New York, Simon and Schuster; London, Lorrimer, 1968).

The 400 Blows, trans. David Denby (New York, Grove Press, 1969).

The Adventures of Antoine Doinel: Four Autobiographical Screenplays, trans. Helen G. Scott (New York, Simon and Schuster, 1971).

The Wild Child, trans. Linda Lewin and Christine Lemery (New York, Washington Square Press, 1973).

Day For Night, trans. Sam Flores (New York, Grove Press, 1975).

The Story of Adèle H, trans. Helen G. Scott (New York, Grove Press, 1976).

The Last Metro, ed. Mirella J. Affron and E. Rubinstein (New Brunswick, Rutgers, 1985).

A total of 12 issues of *L'Avant-Scène Cinéma* have been devoted to Truffaut. A full list may be found in No. 389 (Feb. 1990), which contains the script of *The Woman Next Door*.

Books on Truffaut in English

Allen, Don, *Truffaut* (New York, Viking; London, Secker and Warburg, Cinema One series, 1974; 2nd edition as *Finally Truffaut*, 1985).

Braudy, Leo, (ed.), *Focus on Shoot the Piano Player* (New Jersey, Prentice-Hall, 1972).

Crisp, C.G., *François Truffaut* (London, November Books, 1972).

Insdorf, Annette, *François Truffaut* (New York, Twayne Publications, 1977). Truffaut himself considered that Insdorf's was the best book on his work.

Monaco, James, *The New Wave: Truffaut, Godard, Chabrol, Rohmer, Rivette* (Oxford University Press, 1976).

Petrie, Graham, *The Cinema of François Truffaut* (New York and London, Tantivy Press, 1970).

Wall, James M., *Three European Directors* (Truffaut, Fellini, Buñuel) (Michigan, Eerdmans, 1973).

Walz, Eugen P., *François Truffaut, a Guide to References and Resources* (Boston, G.K. Hall, 1982).

Among the numerous books in French, particular mention should be made of Gilles Cahoreau, *François Truffaut, 1932–1984* (Paris, Julliard, 1989), the only biography of Truffaut to date and especially interesting on his childhood and youth.

Acknowledgements

I would like to thank the British Film Institute Stills, Posters and Designs department and the Joel Finler Collection for the photographs provided, which were originally issued to publicise or promote films or TV material made or distributed by the following companies, to whom I gratefully offer acknowledgement: Les Films du Carrosse, SEDIF, Les Films de la Pléiade, Vineyard Films Ltd, Artistes Associés, Produzioni Associate Delphos, Valoria Films, Fida Cinematografica, Cinetel, Columbia, PECF, PIC, Andrea Films, SEDIF, TF1, Films A2, Soprofilms.

Index